THE POUNCE THEORY

THE
POUNCE
THEORY

How to Create Your
Opportunities in life

BLAZE BHENCE

iUniverse, Inc.
Bloomington

The Pounce Theory
How to Create Your Opportunities in life

iUniverse books may be ordered through booksellers or by contacting:

iUniverse
1663 Liberty Drive
Bloomington, IN 47403
www.iuniverse.com
1-800-Authors (1-800-288-4677)

ISBN: 978-1-4502-9722-6 (sc)
ISBN: 978-1-4502-9725-7 (ebk)

Printed in the United States of America

iUniverse rev. date: 02/22/2011

To Cheryl—my soul mate, life partner, and best friend—who has stuck by my side through thick and thin. Thank you for listening to my dreams and corralling my efforts to reap a beautiful life together.

Contents

Acknowledgments

There are too many people to thank; however, I have a few who—knowingly or not—helped contribute to this book whom I would like to individually acknowledge.

Helga and Axel, you have both always believed in me and inspired me to endure and conquer. I have seen your personal struggles, and you have seen all mine. Thank you for allowing me to learn while guiding me to make the right choices.

Kira and Meaghan, you two have inspired, driven, and compelled me to always do more. These are the same two who have contributed to much of my hair loss as well. Without them, life would not be so good.

Chris Miller, my best man and an inspiration. Your willpower, perseverance, and results-oriented personality are unique features that are admired. You have inspired me to achieve more in life than if I had lived without your encouragement and persistent enthusiasm to make me do the ridiculous.

Chris and Michelle Hoskins, motivators and inspirations to both my wife and me. You've saved me from numerous mistakes and have shown me the light when it comes to personal growth and when to pounce on life's opportunities.

Mike Petran, Audrey Eisner-Holler, Sue Lansil, and the others who made me ride my bike for hours and days past my limits and who spoke to me about always pushing. You have inspired me and helped me increase my inner strength. You also motivated me to write *The Pounce Theory* based on the conversations had during many of our bike rides.

Introduction

This book is designed to provide each and every reader with the insight to recognize when an opportunity arises and the ability to take advantage and maximize that opportunity. Just as a cat stalks its prey, there is a moment when the feeling is just right to pounce. There is a moment when the cat's tail begins to slide back and forth, the ears go back, and the head drops down even farther. It's in that very moment—that split second—when the pounce is being contemplated.

When opportunities present themselves, you need to be in a position to take advantage of those moments and pounce. *The Pounce Theory* will explain how to win in life, not by blind luck or overexertion, but by determining the exact time to move when life hands you an opportunity. Whether you are wanting to climb the corporate ladder, seeking the next move to grow your own business, looking for work, or studying to prepare for the working world, the pounce is the key to exploiting your opportunities and benefiting as much as possible. Whether you are single or married, the pounce is a primary factor in getting what you want out of relationships. Just about everything you do in your daily life can be orchestrated. If you can guide the outcome by controlling the tempo, you can influence a situation dramatically. This emphasis on the timing and how that will affect the outcome of every situation is the focus of this book.

You may have read motivational books before or even attended self-help seminars. Many of these books and seminars discuss the fundamentals that we all need to remember when closing a sale or asking for greater things in life. While these reviews can be beneficial, unless the basics become instinctual, you can easily lose focus on what behaviors you need to practice daily. *The Pounce Theory* is not a book that focuses on the basics, but rather it focuses on the instincts. Instinctually, we all pounce on opportunities when we deem it appropriate. However, we often do not think about the pounce ahead of time to the point where we maximize the effectiveness of our pounce. Setting up the pounce is as important as the act of the pounce itself. The proper pounce works best with optimal timing. *The Pounce Theory* discusses how to attack the opportunities in life, at the right time, in the right way, to maximize your intended goals.

If you invest in the stock market a week before it crashes, your timing is bad. If you ask a girl to go out with you after she is married, your timing is bad. If you run a marathon by bolting out as fast as you can at the sound of the starting gun, you will burn out and possibly not even finish the race. Timing is everything. Likewise, if you time things right, ask for desires at the right time, and think before you act, life may present unbelievable results.

The pounce theory is not a method or thought process designed to manipulate situations and people. Rather, it is a way to effectively assess your priorities and desires and then set up the manner and timing that will most likely bring the best results to meet your goals. The pounce theory is not for the type *A* personalities who need control over every situation. Nor is it a method whereby everyone wins and we all go skipping down the gold-lined road happily ever after. The pounce theory is a method you can use to monitor a situation, assess the direction it is moving, formulate the correct mindset, and act by taking the appropriate steps to ensure your needs are met, and hopefully, it will result in a win for as many involved as possible.

Success is not measured by how much money one makes, what kind of car one drives, or even social status within a small sector of the world. Success is based on happiness and contentedness within oneself, as well as a feeling of getting what is desired in a manner that can be consistently repeated to ensure further successes will be forthcoming. Enacting the pounce theory consistently will ensure success in personal, scholastic, work, and recreational environments throughout your life. Enjoy reading

The Pounce Theory, and then enjoy reaping the benefits of life as they come, when they come.

How to Use This Book

The Pounce Theory is broken up into individual chapters regarding various aspects of life that we may or may not go through. The first part of the book deals with work and work-related issues. Setting up the pounce for a work situation is an entirely different process than when setting up for romance. At work, we deal with internal and external politics. A thorough understanding of corporate politics and of how the boss determines your value is critical to moving forward in your field and your career. Conversely, when looking to enhance your romantic life, politics and manipulation should not be characteristics used to further your efforts.

The chapters are partitioned out so that you, the reader, can read sections pertinent to the present time in your life to best suite your needs. There is not much gained from reading about work issues and the correct time to pounce for your career when you are in school and have two more years before you'll even begin thinking of entering into the workforce. Conversely, there may be no need to read about school or romance issues if you are married and have been working for quite some time, with no desire for going back to school.

Looking at the world from the viewpoint of the events and situations around yourself and learning how to use these real-time situations to better your personal situation is an important practice. The remainder of the book speaks to more specific surroundings and thus more specific behaviors that you can recognize as well as exhibit to maximize the pounce theory, which will maximize your desired outcomes.

The last chapters relating to common daily or routine tasks, such as shopping and traveling, relate to many readers, either on the side of being the shopper or traveler, or the other side of how to deal with shoppers and travelers. Either way, whether you are on one side of the situation or the other, it is good to understand how behaviors of other lend to situations that you can take advantage of.

For the reader who has found value in the pounce theory and desires to read to gain more understanding, you may be interested in reading chapters that do not appear to pertain directly to your circumstances in life, as they may pertain to others around you. This can provide insider knowledge about why these other people in your life operate the way they do in their situations. You may be able to help them further themselves. You may be able to understand them better and thus develop a more advantageous relationship with them.

The pounce theory is not about manipulation of people based on the situation they are in; it is about manipulation of behaviors so that relationships and desires you have are maximized. People feel manipulated when a relationship is one-sided or situations are more advantageous for one party over the other. A proper pounce is one where a situation or circumstance is manipulated to be very advantageous to you, yet at the same time, it allows everyone involved to feel that the end result was a benefit to all. We all hear about striving for the "win-win" solution. The pounce theory is merely a way in which you can view behaviors of others to observe rhythms, cadences, and patterns in people and use those observations to maximize your desires and hopefully maximize a successful solution for.

The General Pounce

We go through life learning and then growing from what we learn. We are often surprised when a disaster strikes or tragedy hits close to home, yet in hindsight, most of these disasters were bound to happen and were somewhat predicable.

The circle of life and the circle of history are very similar. As the old cliché goes, the only two certainties in life are death and taxes. So why are we so surprised by deaths? Why are we so surprised when the economy goes into a downturn? Why are we so surprised when a natural disaster strikes in our region? These are unfortunate incidences that occur on a semiregular basis, yet at unpredictable times. And even with theses unfavorable incidents, opportunities are up for grabs. So how can we prepare for these situations and be ready to pounce on the opportunities that arise?

Here are examples of two of the best cases of incidental opportunities I have seen—one that was not capitalized on, and one that was. In August 29, 2005, Hurricane Katrina hit Louisiana and caused a great deal of flooding and damage, mostly to the city of New Orleans. Over one thousand people died in this tragic natural disaster. Though Katrina was one of the worst hurricanes to ever hit the United States of America, dozens of hurricanes smash into the Gulf states every year. Though some years are worse than others, we all know that hurricanes have a season and they inevitably will hit cities across the Eastern Seaboard and in the Gulf states every year. So what could have been done about this, you might ask. Well nothing could have fully stopped the inevitable damage. Perhaps better planning could have saved hundreds of lives. Though then-Mayor Ray Nagin predicted that the storm surge would likely topple the levee system, it was difficult to fully comprehend the scale of damage and lives lost due to the levees collapsing. However, what was predictable was that hurricanes would hit the United States and that every five years or so the United States will have a very devastating hurricane season. With this knowledge, you would hope the government would recognize this pattern and at least prepare a PR campaign to show that the government cares.

Immediately following the devastating hurricane, Washington DC officials did very little to help the victims of the hurricane. President George Bush relied on FEMA and other agencies and their staffs to do the right things and help the people. President Bush was quickly lambasted for his lackadaisical approach and was criticized as not caring for the poor and afflicted. The PR nightmare lasted for months and was a sore spot for the president for the rest of his term. Could this have been avoided?

Knowing that these tragedies are reoccurring, if Washington had better planned for the inevitable, they could have looked like heroes, even with the same results. After Katrina hit, New Orleans flooded, and approximately thirty thousand people rushed to the Louisiana Superdome for shelter and high ground. These people were stranded without food and clean water for days. No one could get to them, and they had no way out. The scene was bleak for many in need. Eventually, FEMA and other agencies proceeded past the fallen trees and the flooded streets and rescued the stranded thousands, but only after frustrating days with no amenities, food, or water.

Had President Bush taken action at the time to demonstrate compassion, his legacy may have been much different. What would have happened if he would have flown to the Superdome in a helicopter and stayed on the Superdome grounds until the last person left? Could you imagine the image: the president flies in and says, "I will be the last to leave. Save these stranded people." The Secret Service agents would have surrounded the president. He would never have been in trouble. He would have stayed in a suite within the Superdome and would not have had any concerns for safety or food and water. However, the media would not have seen the comforts, but rather the gesture of "I am here for the people, and I will not leave until they are all safe." What would that have done for the people—and for the president's legacy?

This is one example of a predictable pounce. No one can know where the next year's hurricanes will hit and how severe they will be, but what we do know is that in the next five years, there will probably be an opportunity to help hurricane victims, earthquake victims, tornado victims, etc., in various parts of the nation. One can devise a plan to swoop in and be "the savior." The government can plan for the predictable pounce whereby, for a few natural disasters, not only will they have FEMA, the Red Cross, and other agencies available, but also they will have the president and others available to the people for a PR boost.

So you're not the president of the United States. How can you take advantage of a predictable pounce? Here is an example of a successful pounce performed by a very dear and close friend. He started his adult life with $500 in his pocket after college. He lived on the floor of a friend's house and didn't know what he was going to do with his life. Within twenty years, he was worth $124 million, had thirteen Ferraris and muscle cars, and lived in a beautiful home on the oceanfront.

I asked him what his secret to success was. My friend stated, "It's all about timing." He went on to explain. Soon after he had graduated college, he asked his fraternity brothers to chip in and invest in an apartment building. Thirty-five of them pooled their money together and invested and renovated a four-unit apartment complex. After relandscaping, recarpeting and repainting, they raised the rents and sold the property for almost double the initial amount paid. Though on a small scale, each individual didn't make a whole lot of money, they all doubled their money and thus were able to invest and repeat the success. They repeated these efforts four times, and though commissions and profits were not significant, what was significant was the success they had. Then the economy turned and the markets plummeted. Along with the downturn came the collapse of the savings and loan institutions. With the savings and loan debacle, many banking institutions had real estate portfolios that were too large. All the foreclosed properties were coming back to the bank.

Now it may seem like anyone can take advantage of this situation. Hardly. If you walk into a bank with many foreclosure properties in their inventory, the bank will still be very reluctant to sell properties to you for pennies on the dollar. If you have no real estate experience and no experience in turning properties from distressed to success, the banks will not sell you the property you're hoping to buy for low cost. The banks know that most likely you will not be able to sustain the property, and within a short time, they will get the property back on their books.

However, my friend had positioned himself in the real estate environment to show that he was able to turn properties from distressed to successful properties in short order. He had a portfolio of four or more properties that he had strong involvement with. He was able to demonstrate that he could manage the apartments he wished to take on. The banks were able to go through his portfolio and feel comfortable with selling him distressed properties that had been mismanaged. My friend was able to purchase $4 million worth of properties for less than $800,000. He turned the units into profitable properties, which fueled even greater success.

My friend sees the value of always positioning yourself for the inevitable. It is inevitable that the markets will flourish over time, but within those long periods of time, there will be downturns that everyone can take advantage of. It is inevitable that natural disasters will occur in almost every region in the world. It is inevitable that deaths will occur and taxes will come due. There are many incidents in life that are inevitable. Understand the ebb and flow of these times. Understand the nuances that stem from these events, and prepare yourself for them. The power of the pounce is to be prepared and positioned for the right opportunity at the right time. The predictable pounce is the best opportunity you can have under dire circumstances. Face the inevitable head-on; it's what life is all about. Prepare for the future disasters, grieve when they arrive, and then take advantage of the opportunity their arrival presents. Just as seeds sprout when the forest burns down, you can grow after the fire rampages your world.

Have you ever gone through a period of time, a period of life, when you became more reaction based, rather than proactive? Most people go through at least half of their lives in this mode; many are 100 percent in the reactionary mode. This mode is what is classically termed as living in your "comfort zone." The comfort zone is a place where most of us have resided at various stages of our lives for many reasons.

We start in a world where we are told to go to school. Once in school, our days are planned for us and our homework assignments dictate our evening lives to a great extent. We rarely break from the pattern until we are in our late teens, early twenties, or even later in life, depending on how much schooling we choose to undertake. For most of our formative years, we are given a plan, and few questions are asked. Occasionally, we participate in an extracurricular activity. These can be quite time consuming at first, yet soccer, baseball, band, cheerleading, etc., generally consist of a couple practices during the week and the big day on the weekend when we are consumed for a few hours. At first this makes the lifestyle seem hectic; however, a routine begins, and these extracurricular activities become routine or comfortable. We settle into a comfort zone quickly to ensure that we can cope with life once again.

Decision making is minimal for the first eighteen years of our lives. The first major change in this pattern comes at the age when we decide we are ready for our first job. Then life begins getting complicated. We go through getting a new job, new career, settling down, starting a family, and watching the process start over again for our offspring. Other obligations—such as rent or mortgage payments, car payments, clothing costs, credit card debts, etc.—seem to suddenly pile on top of our life. Work the takes place of school for many, yet the full-time job is much more flexible and different from school. Gone are the days where our life is laid out for us to react to. Some work forty years at the same company and retire. Others jump from one job to another. The book *The Economics of Earnings*, by Solomon W. Polachek and W. Stanley Siebert, presents a study showing that the UK population between age sixty and sixty-four had worked an average of 6.9 jobs; in the United States, this number for the same population equals 10.5 jobs. An average between these two figures corresponds to 8.7 jobs in a lifetime. Through the late 1990s, job jumping became more predominant in our society; however, as soon as the dot-com boom went bust so did the job-jumping trend. For most people, staying the course is what is in store for them.

Now for the fun part! Life is not all that dreary. Although we can generalize and compartmentalize life in a few categories, the real adventure begins when we make positive changes in our lives that further our career, family, social network, as well as bring us to a more satisfactory level of living.

We don't enter our careers because we have to. We have choices, and we make those depending on the offers we get and the matches we take. We find a mate and marry, not because we have to or we are told to, but because we feel we've found a soul mate, a life partner whom we can create a life together with. The days of arranged marriages and vocations chosen depending upon what your father or mother did for a living are becoming less and less commonplace in the world. Most Westernized civilizations allow women to enter the workforce if they choose to. Men and women can marry whom they choose, if they choose to do so. Some choose to stay single for many years. Others choose alternative lifestyles.

With technological advancements, careers, sports, recreation, and travel, among other activities, have changed considerably. With these advancements, amusement parks have become more adventurous. Sports like skydiving, bungee jumping, paragliding, mountain biking, and jet skiing have become more commonplace. Travel to far destinations is now considered low cost and time efficient for many corporate and even personal traveling. We are seeing society become more worldly and adventurous.

On the flip side, marriages are more likely to end before "death do us part," jobs are more likely to last for years rather than decades, and next-door neighbors are more likely strangers than best friends. As the world becomes smaller due to technology, the world becomes more spread apart by people socializing in Internet chat rooms instead of by "hanging-out" with the neighbors. These changes in the world and our society have altered how we interact with people. How we choose to live is becoming more complicated with every passing year.

How we cope with change is fundamental to how we cope with life itself. Life is full of changes. We can choose to change with it, or we can make life change with our desires. The pounce theory discusses how to assess your environment, understand your desires, and seize the moment to obtain your goals. For one to do that, a higher state of consciousness needs to be developed. We're not talking about some Zen religious passage we need to take. There will be no meditating required. However, a higher state of consciousness describes a general astuteness with your environment, the people around you, and the current state of events that can help you propel you into your dreams.

The State of Consciousness

Consciousness of one's surroundings is a paramount step in succeeding with the pounce and achieving your goals. A state of consciousness when you know your surroundings and use the moment to help others or yourself is amazing to be involved in. It takes practice, astute observation, thought, and creativity to master a true state of consciousness where you can truly control most situations.

Have you ever wanted to make a right turn, but the car in front of you stopped for the red light in the middle of the lane, preventing you from squeezing by and turning? If only that driver would have been more considerate, perhaps he or she would have realized that being in the right lane means you should stop as far left as possible so that others may squeeze by and not be inconvenienced. This would have allowed you to make your right turn quicker and get to your destination sooner, therefore getting off the roadway sooner, which reduces emissions for all—a benefit that all of society could enjoy. However, the person in front, clogging the lane, does not think of these things, and is probably not thinking of much more than what he or she will do when they arrive at their destination.

This is just one example of people who are not in the state of consciousness about their surroundings. Clearly, if the other person was to stop on the left portion of the lane, it would benefit not only you, as the other driver, but all the people on the road and all the citizens in the region, including the driver in front. However, due to a low sense of consciousness, the driver in front has made everyone's life a bit more difficult.

Consciousness of your surroundings is not a task that can to be performed 100 percent of the time. However, consciousness of your surroundings should take place every time you walk into a new room, every time you see someone again, meet someone new, or venture out into the world. Many of us tend to be conscious of the rest of the world to a limited extent. For example, we all know that appropriate attire is protocol for going to any event. If you are going to a formal party, only formal wear is appropriate. Someone dressed in shorts at a formal party would be noticed as an exception. At a spectator sport, such as a baseball or football game, one would look completely out of place in formal attire. In general, we dress for the occasion. It is at these events that we meet people who can alter our lives. Why risk looking out of place and foolish, when you can possibly lose opportunities in life?

The reason you may lose opportunities by dressing completely out of place is that others are conscious of what you wear. In fact, to a great degree, most of us are more conscious of what others wear than of what we choose to wear. When we look at others, we pass judgments on them based as to what they wear, how they carry themselves, their smile (or lack thereof), and other miscellaneous features. We feel bonded or we are repulsed by others depending on what we see, often within the first few moments. It is believed that, on average, one has between seven to ten seconds to make a first impression. This seven to ten second buffer often starts before the actual first greeting. The seconds start when you walk up to someone, when you walk up to the podium—whenever the other person first sees you. It may be a group of girls pointing at you without your knowledge. It may be a group of decision makers looking to find the person they feel they need to engage. Whoever begins the introduction does not particularly matter. More important is the knowledge that you have roughly ten seconds from the first moment someone lays eyes on you and their first impression.

What does this mean, you may ask? What do consciousness and first impressions have to do with the pounce theory or getting what you want out of life? Well here is where it begins. By being conscious of your surroundings, we can see the importance of looking good, smiling, and generally looking like you are a person others want to be around. It is here where the pounce begins. If you are standoffish or portray yourself as someone who many do not wish to associate with, or if you appear lackadaisical and lackluster, you may lose opportunities in life. You will not be positioning yourself to take advantage of potential opportunities down the road.

What you see in other people is just as important as what people think of you at the first get-go. Most of us walk through life meeting others and allowing a relationship to start or end depending mostly on coincidence and commonalities. If you have a bit in common with someone, you assimilate to them and create more conversation. Usually finding commonalities relies on the circumstance you are in, introductions, and coincidence. We all have our differences and our commonalities with others. Finding the commonalities and minimizing the barriers is key to leaving a good impression—and in the end, setting ourselves up for what we want.

Consciousness begins by knowing your surroundings. Understanding where you are and who is around you are the first pieces you need to consider. Are you in a crowded room, a courtyard with people all around, a conference hall with hundreds of people walking about? Or are you in an intimate setting with one or two other individuals, perhaps a meeting, a carpool, or an interview? You need to ensure that you are projecting the right image for the setting.

In a one-on-one setting or a setting with just a few people in a room, your focus needs to be shifted to the other and off yourself. Eye contact is crucial. Look at others directly without staring. Your stance is important as well; stand erect and facing the other party. Turning sideways appears as if you are excluding individuals and is a turn off to others. Project your voice, but do not shout or speak too loudly. Your demeanor should be polite, yet direct. These are the types of characteristics other individuals are impressed with or turned-off by within the first ten seconds. Your body language speaks volumes before your mouth even opens. Utilize your body to converse the right things about you.

Consciousness about yourself is important, however, consciousness about others goes even further. Now that you are dressed appropriately for the situation you are in and you have the walk and talk of someone who is powerful, it is time to show humility. Humility is the foundation to success. Overbearing individuals tend to push others away. Secondly, an overbearing person appears to have ulterior motives. When you see an overbearing person, you know they want something and thus your defenses are already set to full shield. When a humble person asks you for a favor, you feel grateful they asked you and generally you will be more willing to help them. With this in mind, take the high road. Go in with humility. If the negotiation does not go your way, the time to pounce will appear and a strong defense will win you the battle. Go into battle with your guns drawn and everyone gets hurt.

Coming across with humility can be tricky; however, you may be surprised at how easy it can be. Almost every single person on the face of this earth loves to talk, hear about, and focus on him or herself. In the book *How to Win Friends and Influence People*, Dale Carnegie wrote that when attempting to get a building constructed, he could ask for upfront money from numerous people and no one would give a penny. However, if he offered that their names would be on the building, suddenly everyone would be willing to pitch in money. Everyone loves to hear their name. They want you to be interested in them, in their lives. People want to talk about themselves. With such an easy entrance, why not use it to your advantage. Whether you are with old friends or new acquaintances, the first priority should be the stories of the other person. You can start by asking simple questions, such as "How are you doing?" and "What are you doing today?" But soon after they give the answers, use these to lead into more pointed questions about themselves. This is where consciousness is important to practice.

When someone begins to converse with you, you can idly listen, or you can actively listen and look for more discussion topics. Usually, there are smaller stories that can be elaborated on, if only someone cared for the details. Be that person. Ask for details of the stories that are presented.

A person will tell you many things just for the asking. A person will tell you many more things, if you just look. Look at what he or she is wearing. Glance at the makeup. Observe the hair: the part, the coloring, the styling.

Look at their shoes. Also, observe the posture, the hand gestures, the eye contact, the facial expressions, and the body movements. These are all attributes you look for unconsciously; now start to bring these things into your conscious.

I have gained a better understanding of nonverbal communication through my personal observations, courses on behavioral patterns, and training received from various government agencies. Use your own personal observations to steer a conversation to your needs, at the appropriate time. Listen to others, try not to interrupt, and gauge the appropriate time to pounce and get what you want. You may need a simple favor or have a simple question. Or perhaps you need considerable help or money. Knowing when to pounce, knowing when to ask your questions, is key to getting your desired outcome. The following behaviors and characteristics are some traits to look for when speaking to someone. Observe these attributes in people, and you will see consistent tendencies and habit displayed by most people.

Hairstyle
Is the hair styled, combed, disheveled, colored, etc.?

A person into self-care and proper grooming usually wants to be noticed and praised. Unkempt hair is a sign that, at least on that particular day, they may feel down to earth and may not fall for lavish praise.

Colored hair tends to show that the person wants to preserve their youth or wants to be an individual. They took time to be noticed, so notice them in a positive manner.

Fancy hair parts, braids, or other grooming tasks means that the person takes time to care for himself or herself and thus appreciates others noticing the efforts. Compliment the hair.

Clothing
Some people wear T-shirts with corporate insignias, others wear designer label, and others wear plain clothing. Notice what type of garments they are sporting.

Wearing a corporate T-shirt may mean that the person is not placing a high emphasis on their clothing on that particular day. Complimenting their clothing may sound ridiculous. Of course, the shirt may have some significance, and asking what the logo means may lead to a story the person wants to tell.

Some wear designer labeled clothing. This usually means the individual has taken time in their shopping and the choosing of their outfits. Complimenting them on their decision will go a long way. An acknowledgment that the time they took to shop was worthwhile is a reward others appreciate.

Lastly, some wear no labels or logos. This may mean the individual is exactly that—an individual. It may also mean that the person is not tied to a designer label or a certain look. Complimenting their clothing tastes may not hurt, but it will most likely not be a major topic of discussion, and therefore it may be seen as a minor compliment to the person.

Scent

Some individuals are into aromas and smelling good. Some do not care as much. Try and notice if there is a fragrance associated with a person. If detected, let the person know that he or she is wearing a pleasant cologne or perfume. Manufactured aromas tend to be used by individuals who care what others think and want to impress others. Ask what fragrance they use and compliment it. Noticing this with these types of individuals can be very beneficial.

Too much of an aroma can mean a cover-up. Often, people who either have not bathed in over a day or are covering up another odor, such as alcohol, overuse colognes or perfumes for masking. Mentioning the person's fragrance could cause embarrassment. Be cautious with a compliment and just try not to sneeze.

Posture

Posture is a topic that most people ever discuss; however, it is a very noticeable feature. An individual who slouches may not think highly of him or herself or may not care much of what others' opinions are of him or her. Compliments regarding appearance may fall on deaf ears. Compliments of the person's thoughts, ideas, or other mind-related areas are better to focus on.

A person with a good posture generally thinks well of him or herself. This individual is usually confident and outgoing. A good posture tends to be indicative of an individual who has a mission and a goal in life. Ask about those goals. You will notice the conversation will go far.

Smile

It has been said that a smile alone can get you anything you want. People love others who smile. A smile brightens everyone's day and can make the difference between a positive opinion and a negative opinion of others. Acknowledging someone's smile can be more powerful than just smiling back. State that they have a great smile, and the person is putty in your hands.

If a person tends not to smile, this may be for a few reasons. Perhaps the individual is saddened by a loss in the family or illness. Perhaps the individual is contemplating a serious issue and is distracted. Or perhaps the individual is not the jolly sort and feels no need to smile.

Sadness or illness of any kind is very discomforting to all involved. Asking what is troubling the individual and comforting him or her will usually help tremendously. This separates you from the thousands who ask "How you doing?" without really caring about the answer. Be there for a person and comfort them during a troubling time, and you will always be regarded as a friend.

Otherwise, smile at people when you see them and even when you are speaking to them on the phone. When you smile, your voice inflection changes. During my first sales training course, I was told to talk on the phone in front of a mirror and make sure your smile does not fade. I quickly learned that smiling while speaking on the phone can lead to more pleasant conversations. Clearly, if a smile works over the phone, it will certainly help when speaking to individuals in person. Be careful with fake smiles, but try and smile as often and as appropriately as you can.

Eye Contact

Eye contact is imperative to any conversation. Maintain eye contact. If your eyes wander, it shows that you are distracted and uninterested in the other person. It may not be true; however, it is the perception. Lack of eye contact can mean shyness, lack of trust, being uncomfortable within the setting, or interest lying elsewhere.

If someone avoids of eye contact, you need to help them focus. Perhaps suggesting a different place to talk could ease the individual. A change in the surrounding, away from crowds or others that are causing distractions may do the trick. If their interest is elsewhere, most likely they will allude to that, and you need to be sensitive and allow room for them to seek out that interest. Shyness or an uncomfortable setting can be overcome by moving to a more secluded area in or out of the room. If the person does not trust you or feels awkward because of you particularly (e.g., an ex-spouse situation), be sensitive to these issues and walk lightly on various topics. Do not confront the individual or demand action from them. Their defenses will shoot up, and they will flee or fight. This is not an area where you can pounce and win or stand to gain anything except anger.

There are many books and research papers written on human behaviors, but you do not need to be an expert in this area to be observant and cognizant of your surroundings. People have "buttons" to push for both positive and negative reactions. A little observation of the way a person carries themselves can help with bringing out and steering a conversation. Conversation generally will run a course; you have the ability to steer and conduct the conversation in a manner that will be pleasant and beneficial to all parties involved. When a conversation is pleasant, people desire more conversation and will seek out your company later. This can reap rewards in the immediate future or down the road. Either way, it will come back in a positive manner. Be conscious of others and their behaviors—as they are of yours. Noticing and mentioning these behaviors shows that you are in tune with your surroundings and in touch with others.

At Work

Business Relationships

Relationships are extremely complicated matters whereby two or more individuals are engaged in some sort of personal or business connection. This section of the book will be focused on business relationships. Romantic relationships and marriage will be discussed in later chapters.

Business relationships are simpler relationships tied together by a single need to succeed in one task: create or keep a successful business that can sustain a living for the parties involved. Unlike a romantic relationship that can have many desires and goals, in business, the main goal is to be successful, however that is defined.

In all relationships, the wise expression "pick your battles" should be remembered in the heat of the moment. A business relationship, or any relationship for that matter, is a partnership. You are together in a venture, striving for a common goal. Keeping this in mind is often difficult when the path to that goal is different for the parties involved. The important thing to remember is that the ultimate goal is the same, though the methodology may be different. With that in mind, you must remind your partner(s) of that fact.

When discussing a method for success in a business relationship, hopefully more often than not you will be in agreement with the overall path to success. Should an occasion arise when you are in disagreement, it is imperative that you take a step back and assess the situation. Without this important pause, rash decisions get made, egos get in the way, and often times a heartfelt decision is made as opposed to a thought-out business decision. This effectively reduces your pounce ability in the future and can create further stresses on the relationship. This is one time when it may be appropriate to get into your comfort zone. Dealing in your comfort zone can ease your mind and thus allow you to project your issues in a manner that will be more conducive to acceptance. When you deal with others in your comfort zone, you are dealing with others the way they are accustomed to dealing with you. You have a manner in which they feel comfortable with you, otherwise the relationship would never have begun. Listen, think win-win, and figure out how to use the pounce to fulfill your desires.

So what does it mean to bring the conversation into your "comfort zone"? Basically, bring the parties to your level. Once there, the room is yours. To do this, you may need to take a breath and ask for a moment. Perhaps that could mean a bathroom break, or perhaps that could mean a recess for the evening or for lunch. However much time you need, you need to ask for it and then utilize this time to constructively set forth your agenda in a manner that everyone will listen to. That may mean writing down your thoughts, it may mean formulating a speech in your head so you can confidently take the podium when you return to the bargaining room, it may even mean asking others who share your opinion to join in on the negotiation. Whatever you feel most comfortable doing, that is the state you must create. I've often seen people utilize e-mail effectively to convey their feelings; whatever works for you, make it happen. Now you are in your "comfort zone." This is where your pounce will be most effective.

Once you have taken the time to formulate your reasoning, you can convey it in a proper and professional manner, which will hopefully allow you to get your way, or at the very least, be heard. The pounce should not be made in the heat of the moment in a boardroom if one can help it. Always ask to be excused, take your time, and then pounce in your most effective way. Most people will respect your desire to not make rash decisions and thus will respect you methodologies more, just for that reason alone.

Sales to Outside Customers

So much of what we do at work is negotiation, whether for a sale, a raise, or simply delegating a task. Negotiation is a perennial struggle throughout our daily lives, with customers, bosses, and even our own children.

No one will insist on negotiating more than outside customers. These will be the most difficult negotiations you will face. Timing and the pounce are the most important strategy pieces for selling to a customer, though many sales organizations, sales consulting firms, and sales training courses state otherwise.

"The key to selling is to demonstrate a need for your product." While this is certainly very real and true, timing is even more important. No one "needs" a record player. Demonstrating a need for this out of date device would be very difficult. If your product is out of date or the economy is weak, it will be very difficult to sell your product. So can this be used as an excuse whenever your product is not selling? No. You need to find create the perfect timing. Let the customer know that the time is now for your product(s) or service(s). So if the record player you are trying to sell seems out of date, you need to create the illusion that the time is now for analog devices and their superior sound quality to come back. Now is the time for true audiophiles and musicians to begin recording back onto vinyl. Now is the time to pounce. This will have your customers seeing the need for your product, but more importantly, they will feel compelled to purchase *now*—while the timing is right.

Many salespeople have faced the dilemma of customers who see the value of their product, have the desire for the product, but cannot purchase for budgetary, formal approval, or other reasons that seem to delay the buying cycle. Yet if the customer is truly compelled to purchase, it's amazing how fast they can get an order signed. Demonstrating the timing of the need is critical. No one delays the buying cycle of food, toilet paper, gas, or other true needs. Clothing is often delayed until there is a need, such as "back-to-school" sales, the new spring or fall looks and sales, or other compelling times. Again, timing is critical. Seeing a movie can wait until it is released to download or pay-per-view if the movie is not demonstrated as a "must see right now" or "see it in larger than life" on the big screen. Virtually all items we buy can be delayed if the timing is not right, Demonstrating that the need is *now* is critical.

So how does one create the proper timing? Sales need to be driven. The key to the successful salesperson is driving customers to timely buying. Typically, any customer interested in listening to a salesperson's pitch has already begun the buying process. That customer already sees the value of the product and may actually feel a need for the product. Unfortunately, that is not enough. There may be a greater need to save money, to wait until a better product comes along, or to get something less expensive or disposable until a "better time." If you can demonstrate the timing of your product is ripe and that there is no better time to buy, you can sell.

The sense of urgency must be driven home. Often this sense of urgency can be made by placing a timeline in the customer's head. There are a number of questions that can be asked to develop this timeline:

- "What if" this product is not purchased soon?
- When will you purchase, and what will you do between now and then?
- Why continue to work in the current mode rather than with new product efficiencies?
- What do you think your competitors are doing?
- How long do you wait until you play catch-up to competition?
- What will your customer's customer think if you do not buy this product?
- Can you afford not to buy this product?
- The longer you wait, the more money you spend through inefficiency and productivity loss. How long can you wait?
- Will your managers or shareholders respect your decision to do nothing and wait?

Understanding the customer's mindset will be critical. Too much pushing will cause your client to push back or walk away. Too little may cause them to think more than they need to and delay the sale.

Typically, these questions can shed light and stir up emotions in potential buyers. Questions can lead people to act. Stating "the time is now" is a demotivator and a push-selling strategy. Most people push back when pushed upon. Leading is a much better approach to selling, and questioning decisions or lack thereof is the best way to lead to a close. Questioning is the key to timing, or the key to the pounce. Once a customer is stifled and cannot answer a question, he or she will be left pondering the consequences of not acting. This will drive them to fact find and get answers.

Often the sales can slip away at this point if you do not stay on top of your game and continue presenting yourself as the main expert. If you allow your customer to seek approval from their superiors, you may lose the deal once they go there. Superiors will often find a way to squash needs when it comes to spending money. This is why you need to be engaged with the final decision maker. Again, asking questions and leading to the close will get you there. Don't ever let a key influencer or gatekeeper do the talking for you to the superiors. If this begins to happen, you need to ask them if they are qualified to convey the message properly. Suggest that perhaps another presentation by you to upper management would be best to demonstrate the product and answer all questions that may arise. Allowing it to slip away into someone else's hands usually will cost you the sale. If you cannot get away with arranging a higher-level meeting, then you must drive them to see you.

"Baffle them with BS" is a common expression. Perhaps "BSing" a client is not the intent, however, confusion may be an ally. If a customer wishes to take your presentation to upper management themselves, this may be the time to actually try and baffle the customer. You need to get to the decision maker. If someone is stopping you, you need to ask questions to get him or her to want to act in your best interest. You need to make the product complex enough so that it will take having you there to straighten everything out and ensure all questions get appropriately answered. If you do this right, you will always be in front of the decision maker, questioning them about waiting any longer to buy your product. This technique will lead to demonstrating timing, and this technique will lead to sales. Again, don't let someone else do your selling for you.

Sales to Inside Organizations

Selling inside your organization is often very different from selling to outside customers; however, there is one thing in common—timing is everything. Here are some examples of internal sales:

- Asking your manager for a promotion or raise
- Promoting an idea or change for the company
- Protecting your organization from budget cuts or personnel cutbacks
- Positioning your organization in an effective way so that the company meets various goals and targets

Internal selling can take many forms and is an integral part of any work function.

There is a very marked difference between negotiation and selling. In a negotiation, you, as the instigator, can always walk away. If you do not like the price, product, or offer enough, you leave the sale on the table for another day.

In negotiations, you are on the offensive asking for a better deal. Selling, in many ways, is defensive by nature, in that if the deal does not go through, you lose. You need to sell people on an idea, concept, or product or you do not gain a thing. Negotiating a promotion or raise in pay can be attempted, but you better have a good place to go if the negotiations fail. In order to get a promotion or raise, you need to sell yourself. This holds true for any internal selling you attempt.

So let's look closer at internal selling. Remember, since these dialogues are not negotiations, there are no fallback positions. You must work at getting the maximum gain possible with the least amount of resistance or provocation. Remember, selling internally takes time and timing. In any selling scenario, you must set the stage. The key to sales of any kind is mutual benefit; if the boss sees the benefit of giving you a raise or promotion, you will receive your request.

It is important to gather intelligence so that you know how best to formulate the sale to present it as a benefit the internal client. One option is to ask other similar organizations where their most difficult challenges lie. Then ask these organizations about their perceptions of your organization to help you gain understanding of your importance. Do not ask these questions randomly—ask a few days after a major project or undertaking has passed. Assess the value of your organization from others, after the need for your assistance has been affirmed. Premature asking will only lead others to question your necessity. You may also want to ask your boss what his or her impression is of you—or better, what he or she feels is needed to promote people within the department. These questions will help set up your pounce, but they should not be direct questions in an attempt for the desired outcome, yet.

To sell yourself to those inside your own company, you must constantly look for the opportune moment to pounce. Walking in to your boss's office when he or she is consumed in a difficult task would certainly not be the most opportune time to sell yourself. Asking colleagues to buy into an idea of yours, needs to be finessed at the right time; otherwise you come out looking like an outcast trying to climb your way up by stepping on others or as a self-absorbed individual trying to say "do it my way."

Whenever you feel like you need to make a change in the way business is conducted by your company or organization, you need to sell your ideas internally. This could be when you ask others to buy into a practice that you believe in, or when you see steps in your work that you can make more efficient. If you have a new way of doing things, a new way of accomplishing goals, or just a new way of dealing with the daily routine, you need to sell these ideas to your peers and your management. But you cannot just get on your soapbox and preach about your ideas; you need to create a *need* for your ideas as well as a desire to have you fix the issues. You need to set an example of what you do that is so different that others should do the same and make it a standard. It may be a process that can be eliminated or increased for the betterment of the organization. Your idea may be as benign as just changing the way you dress for work. Whatever the sell is, you need to establish a reason for the change, show quantifiable results that would benefit the vast majority of the people in the organization, and, finally, an implementation process that makes it all come together easily.

25

Merely stating that you have a great idea will typically fall on deaf ears. People may agree that you have a great idea, but that's usually as far as it goes. Have a good idea, a plan to carry it out, and quantifiable data to show that the idea will work—now you have others not only agreeing that you have a good idea, but willing to implement the solution demonstrated. This is the key to your pounce. When you sell your idea internally, make sure you have thought it through so you can share these three parameters with everyone, not only about the value of the idea, but the ease to conduct the operation, and the results it will get. Once you have established these parameters, stating this to others is the easy part. The pounce is virtually complete.

Selling Yourself to Your Peers

Many feel that there is no need to sell themselves to their peers. They are your friends, or they are not; either way, your peers are your equal and therefore do not need to be sold on you. This is a fatal mistake many make. Your peers will not be your peers forever. Some may climb the corporate ladder and become your boss or at least powerful within your organization or even in the industry. Others may stay in the same position but will be integral to the team that you may be heading some day. Your peers may be your friends, but their role with you in the workplace most likely will change.

Selling yourself to your peers can be a bit tricky. Usually, there is no one moment that you can pounce and create a need for you. There is no active selling to anyone hoping they will stand by your side and help you get promoted. Instead, selling yourself to your peers involves patience and humility. Day by day, you do your job and others do theirs. Yet some days are harder than others. When a peer has a difficult day, this becomes your opportunity to help out. They may need some time off to run an urgent errand. They may need an ear to talk to or run ideas by. The time will come where they could use help, but most likely, will not ask for it. They may not ask you because they do not know you that well. Your peers may not ask for help because their situation involves personal issues that may be inappropriate to discuss with coworkers. Whatever it is they need, it usually does not come out unless you are very close to the individual. You need to draw it out.

These efforts will not only solidify friendships, but they will cast you as a leader and a strong individual whom others respect and could work for in the future. Regardless of circumstances in the future, you will have a team of individuals whom will support you in the long term.

If you take the time to observe those around you, you can tell when an individual is down, overrun, consumed, or distant. These characteristics come out during high stress moments when individuals have multiple issues on their minds. Even if people notice someone struggling, most people will walk by and not ask them about their thoughts. They may think the day is too busy to delve into lengthy conversations about things that do not directly impact their work. However, if you do not take the opportunity to help out a fellow colleague during these times, you miss your pounce. Your pounce is when there is an opportunity, not when you see a shinny, happy, smiling face. When you see someone out of his or her element or who seems to need to talk, take the time to do so. It will get you a long way. Start conservatively and merely ask "You seem preoccupied. Everything okay?" or perhaps "You don't seem to be yourself today. Anything troubling you?" These simple questions usually lead to a pushback response stating everything is fine. If you don't say anything and instead choose to wait patiently in silence, usually the person will start to talk. Often it will only require a few seconds of silence before the other will reveal the troubles they are going through. If you can keep silent and let the other discuss their issues, you can establish yourself as a person they can go to in vulnerable times and in awkward situations. You can become their ear, their idea creator, and their best friend. By being willing to listen, you can create a great friend and supporter. Remember, the pounce does not have to be an active action on your part. Simple silence can go a long way and may be the best pounce possible.

Selling Yourself to Your Chain of Command

Asking others about you or your organization may sound narcissistic or self-absorbed; however, those who are concerned with the well-being of the company should always be questioning the value they present to the company and those inside the company. If you are not asking how you can do a better job, you probably have a lot of growth potential you are unaware of, Ask others in an open way to get both honest feedback and constructive criticism. Generally, you will find that you have room to grow and much improvement can be done to streamline your organization or even your own work habits. However, once you begin to get the feedback and make inroads into these issues, other will see that you are capable of changing and making the work environment a better place for all. This is when the pounce gets set.

Once you have a good sense of value within the company, you can begin to sell yourself, your needs, and your desires. Here is where selling takes patience. In selling, you need to instill a sense of timing and urgency as much as a sense of need. If you have already established a need for your services, you now need to ask open-ended questions about your organization and the value you bring to the table. If your boss questions what you do all day, you are not in a good position to sell yourself. If the boss commends you on your organization or your value in some manner, that's when you know that you are valued. Selling yourself at this time comes easier. You have established value, therefore you have established need. You are needed for your company to grow, or at least for your boss to look good. At this time, you must sell, but not whine about your value.

Selling yourself is merely having a conversation with your manager or managers who can make a difference in your pay grade or your position within the company. The conversation should be pointed and short, yet called for, not just discussed by happenstance in the hallway. If you bring up your good deeds in passing to your manager(s), you sound like you are beating your chest and asking for a pat on the back. Most likely, that will be all you get. If, instead, you request a meeting to discuss your roles and responsibilities, you create a formal time to actively and openly discuss your role and potential career path. This call for a meeting sets up a serious atmosphere in which management can be made aware of your value and your desires. These issues should be put on the table, discussed, and a course of action should come from the meeting.

Management may want you to continue to work on a few areas, or they may realize that you are due for a promotion. If they give you actions to follow, make sure you close them. Make sure you ask for the carrot if you do what is requested. This can be accomplished by simply asking, "If I complete all these tasks or do as you ask, when can I expect a promotion (or raise)?" If, however, management does not have any items that they list for you to improve on, you have all reached the conclusion that you are in-line for the raise or promotion you desire. At this time, you've achieved what you needed to accomplish, now you just need to ask when the reward will transpire. Mission accomplished. The pounce is in setting up the meeting at the right time and ensuring that your request is taken as serious and not as a side note or cooler talk, which comes across as begging.

Negotiations

General Negotiations

Negotiating skills are difficult to master and are rarely found in excellent format, particularly in the Western culture. Populations in the Middle East, Africa, and the Orient have dealt with the art of haggling and negotiation for centuries. Haggling for prices and bartering have been standard practices and a ways of life for many people in these regions. When these cultures clash with that of the Western world, difficulties arise and false perceptions are created.

Negotiations can be beneficial to all parties and can be fun and fulfilling processes to engage in. Often, when a purchase is made, we are disappointed when we find the same or similar item on sale elsewhere. In many countries, there are no prices on products, or if there are, the prices are highly inflated. People "haggle" or negotiate for prices on products. When a haggling process is used, we are not able to tell if we are "taken to the cleaners"; we merely see an inflated price labeled on products and know we got a better deal than the listed price. A feeling of earning the deal prevails when we engage in negotiations.

With large purchases, such as cars, houses, or businesses, negotiating is almost always the approach used to come to a final price. For smaller purchases or maintenance items, it is more customary to pay a price that is posted or labeled on the product in the United Sates. For these smaller purchases or necessity purchases, purchasing for list price may leave a bitter taste when one finds out that a friend received an even better deal. This is where many develop a feeling that they got slighted or got "ripped off." If, instead, we negotiated and learned from our attempts, we could benefit greatly the next time around.

In today's age of technology, the world is becoming used to prices fluctuating and generally dropping significantly, sometimes within months or even weeks. Often a computer on sale is virtually half price within weeks after the initial price offering. However, if we negotiate a price, we can say we earned the deal. If you receive a great deal, you'll feel terrific from the win. Obviously, if the deal is not a great one, you still purchased the product for what you considered fair at the time, and a lesson is learned for the next negotiation process.

It is through these lessons learned that we become better negotiators. It is similar to how we negotiated riding bicycles when we were young. The first few lessons were scary and painful. However, after a few falls, we were able to negotiate bicycling to a decent degree. After even more practice, we mastered it. Negotiating for any sized purchase is much the same, with one exception: negotiation has a timeliness to it. Every negotiation is perishable, and if the product or service is not purchased at a certain time, it most likely will be lost. For this reason, the pounce theory should be used.

If we look at various types of negotiations, we will see a definitive pattern to them. Through studying these patterns, we can learn how to act in a manner that enables the pounce theory to work. Once the pounce is sprung, a successful negotiation can be won.

However, one thing must always be remembered: not all deals *should* be made. A good friend of mine once told me the best deals he ever made were the deals he never made. If he had pushed forward and committed before the appropriate time, he would be as poor as a church mouse—instead, he is one of the richest individuals I know monetarily, psychologically, and spiritually.

If the negotiation does not feel right or is not satisfactory to your liking, the best outcome may be to walk away and search for a better opportunity.

Business Matters

When negotiating with others, we must look at what the other party brings to the table. Dealing across international borders is quite different from negotiating within the United States. However, within the United States, negotiations are different when dealing with commercial entities versus government entities. Regional differences as well as corporate cultures also need to be understood.

Corporate Negotiations

Corporations come in many varieties, sizes, and cultures. Large corporations act and negotiate differently than small entrepreneurial companies. Old corporations, such as IBM and Xerox, negotiate differently than newer corporations, such as Microsoft and Cisco. No one can make a blanket statement as to how to negotiate with all corporations completely. However, there is one thing most corporations have in common: the need to make money. If you can show them a reason to hire you or a reason to purchase from you or your organization that will save them or make them money, you get the deal. You can sell any corporation a $10,000,000 solution if that solution makes the company $10,000,001 the next day. Money is no object if you can demonstrate the value of your product or service and relate that value to bottom-line dollars. They key to corporate negotiation lies within the cost justification.

When first opening a dialogue with a large company, sifting through the internal infrastructure can be the most difficult part of getting to the negotiation. Sales reps often get burnt out on the process of uncovering the correct decision maker. The reason for the burnout is that they put their heart into selling their products or services to everyone in the corporation before they even get close to the decision makers. By the time the runaround gets monotonous, the sales representative gives up and moves on to the next account. Of course, this does not describe a good account manager. The good account managers persist through the minutia until they find the appropriate decision makers. Then the pounce begins.

The pounce cannot begin with just anyone. What tends to happen if you sell your product to the first individual you see is they become a temporary champion of the product. That individual often takes your pitch, shares it with their higher-ups, and leaves it at that. Upon your return, you are informed that management has reviewed the product or service, and they'll get back to you. Your pounce was premature and lost among the shuffle of the great corporate bureaucracy. It is important to make many friends in the organization; however, keep your best for last and make sure everyone knows that you are introducing them to something revolutionary and that a full demonstration or presentation must be made to understand the full potential of what you have to offer.

Government Negotiations

When dealing with various parts of the government, negotiations are generally completely different from those in the commercial world. Whether you are dealing with the United States Government or international governments, negotiations can be challenging, time consuming, and frustrating. Proper timing of introductions, negotiations, spec and bid creations, and final sales are crucial in succeeding with government sales. The pounce must be set up well in advance or failure will be certain.

"Challenging" can be a nebulous term, such as when people say "that's interesting." In government negotiations, challenging refers mostly to the difficulty negotiating the highly political environment, the difficultly finding the decision maker(s), and often the difficultly demonstrating a business need. Government agencies are political, no matter what branch of service they fall under. The more tied to Capitol Hill a firm is, the more that firm can negotiate or conduct business. This applies as well to state and local governments. The closer you are to the core government decision makers, the easier it can be to gain traction for decision making.

Lobbyists and campaign contributors usually get the first crack at influencing where government funds are going. Congress or other agencies, based on specifications given to them from some chosen company, develop their own set of exclusionary specifications behind closed doors. For example, Congress may know they need to approve appropriations for spending on a task like security. However, Congress usually will not know what technologies are available or what exactly is needed. With minimal time and effort, congressional legislators will try and hone down requirements. A Request for Proposal (RFP) is usually sent out to at least three firms that can bid for the work. In order to write the RFP, legislators need to understand what can and cannot be done—basically, how to write the RFP. Often, they will go to a company and ask for details, in this case, security technology specifications. Given the ability to place a raw specification request, a company can specify so many items that in essence, they sole source the spec. In other words, the specification will be written in such a way that only that firm could qualify for the funding since only their product can match the requirement 100 percent.

The pounce is not in responding to the RFP better than anyone else; it is in helping write the RFP itself. Those firms that help create the RFP surely have a better chance of winning and receiving the project funds.

To effectively negotiate in this arena, it helps to be the firm that Capitol Hill is convinced knows about their needs and submits bid specifications to. If you are not, you need to be able to (a) view the requests for quotation, and after review, learn how to adjust to the requirements or (b) challenge the specifications.

Lengthy books have been written on this subject matter and unless you have the time, legal know-how, and patience, you are better off asking consultants who specialize in this field to help. Then you will have a lobbyist in your corner that can help you obtain funding.

Time consumption is another issue when dealing with government agencies. The average sales cycle for most products or projects is six to nine months. If the project is more complicated or is agency-wide encompassing, the sales cycle will tend to extend to around two years. For smaller companies, this lengthy process can be very frustrating and not worth chasing. Some companies feel that they can reduce the sales cycle to less than six months. Often, these companies do not realize government procurement rules and regulations. Usually, no matter how high the decision maker is in the chain of command, they still must go through the procurement process. This process involves a system of checks and balances to ensure no improprieties occur. To do this, the decision maker needs to submit a request for purchase to the procurement officer within the agency. After proper submission of the bid and paperwork, the procurement officer will send out a CBD, a sort of advertisement, letting companies know of the requirement needed. Again, this process can often take as long as six months for the procurement officer to get at least three bids for the project or product. After obtaining three or more bids, the procurement officer can purchase the "best value" product. That term is also nebulous and therefore often is applied to the originator's primary choice. However, the bid process has been completed, and everyone is happy. The number one saying in the government procurement offices that I have dealt with has always been, "We just want to make sure that if *60 Minutes* walked in, they would find nothing."

Lastly, "Look for the money" is a phrase often used in dealing with the government. As mentioned earlier, anyone can sell a $10 million solution to a commercial company, as long as that solution will make $10 million and $1 the next day. If there is a quantifiable value to the company, they will buy. That makes sense, and in a free enterprise market, companies usually procure when it makes sense—otherwise, they will not be in business very long. With the government, you can't sell a solution for $1 even if it can save the taxpayers $10 million by the next day. The reason is that if the agency or detachment does not have the money to spend, they cannot buy anything. Conversely, an agency with excess funds will spend $10 million with a snap of their fingers, especially around the end of the fiscal year, even if they do not need the product or solution. Some agencies and military detachments end up with a large funding surplus. By the end of the fiscal year, if the agency has a "use it or lose it" policy and the organization has money left over, they lose it, and the next year's budget may be reduced to reflect the true money needs of the department. Therefore, to reduce the risk of budget cuts, the agency will spend every penny even if they do not need to. This can happen at any time of the year; however, 90 percent of the panic spending comes in the month of September for the US Government. Foreign governments are not much different, but they often have different fiscal year dates. For most state and local agencies as well as school district and universities, the end of June is the fiscal year end. What this means is that business often does not come from areas that make sense; instead, business comes from where the money is. So to properly negotiate to gain business from the government, one does not necessarily need to chase the agencies that can utilize your product most effectively; rather, you need to learn where the money is and ask for it at the appropriate time.

These practices make government negotiation challenging in many ways. However, understanding them is crucial to gaining access to very large sources of cash. Patience is critical, and the pounce is imperative. Realizing that the sales cycle will take six months or more and that decisions are made in the last months more than in any other month, companies need to canvas agencies and pitch products around the proper timeframe. April through June are the best months to be in front of the customer in the United States Government. Once you have established the contacts and sold the decision makers on your services, procurement has just enough time to run it through their process. Come September, they will have enough time and bids to make a decision, and they will make one quickly. Again, you or need to be engaged once again to ensure the bid is awarded to you. So to recap, for the federal government, April through June are set-up months, and September is pounce time. For state and local agencies, January through March are set-up months, and June is pounce time. You can be much more aggressive in June or September, and you will receive fruits for your labor throughout the year.

International Negotiations

When dealing with various parts of the globe, we need to realize that different cultures negotiate in different ways. Many cultures do not understand other cultures and therefore either have difficulties negotiating or often cannot come to agreements, merely due to lack of understanding. Generally, unless educated, trained, and experienced in different cultures, one tends to view the world through one's own eyes. But not everyone in the world thinks in a uniform way, making international negotiations challenging.

Having grown up in a mixed cultural environment and having been fortunate enough to travel throughout the world for both business and pleasure, I have come to realize firsthand that understanding cultural differences and melding into the culture that you are dealing with will help tremendously in all endeavors of negotiation. Whether you need to order food from a foreign restaurant or are negotiating multimillion dollar deals with other countries, being the "ugly American" and only dealing in the traditional American ways may take you down a losing path.

Let's take a look at the various regions of the world. For simplicity, we will break the world up into six cultural regions; however, it needs to be pointed out clearly that within these regions, there are many subtle differences. The purpose of regionalizing negotiation types is to keep negotiations simple and to better understand when to pounce for your deal. This breakdown is not to stereotype individuals or regions, rather it is being provided to help bring an understanding of cultural differences to the negotiating table. If one needs to understand cultures further, in-depth analysis needs to be conducted into the intimacies of the particular individual(s) you are dealing with.

The six cultural negotiating types can be separated out as follows:

- North American: consisting primarily of the United States and Canada
- European: consisting mostly of the Nordic countries, England, and even Russia and Australia
- Asian: consisting of countries within Asia and Malaysian islands, including India
- Middle Eastern: consisting mostly of Arabic and Muslim nations within the Northern African and Southern European borders, including Pakistan
- Latin: consisting mostly of South America and Latin culture counties, such as Spain, Portugal, and Italy
- Third World: consisting of some Central and South American countries, most of Africa, much of the Caribbean countries, and scattered counties across the globe

Within these regions, cultural differences between one region and another are often misunderstood and misinterpreted. However, there are some generalities that are worth noting.

North American

Pouncing on a deal with a North American is more a matter of demonstrating a need or desire for the product or service. In North America, most people are brought up in a culture where prices are marked in a store or retail location of some kind. If the price is marked down, due to a sale, "Americans" feel they receive a great deal. Otherwise, the price marked on the item is the price to pay, no questions asked. Often if a reference is made as to reducing the price, the clerk in the store does not have the authority to negotiate, and therefore, no negotiation can be conducted. For these reasons, North Americans have more difficulties with negotiation in the retail setting than most other cultures. This also applies to everything from merchant transactions to large purchases, such as property and businesses. A price is set and negotiations are minimal compared to other parts of the world. Deals are based more on initial price offers than in most other countries. To pounce with an American, the best negotiation is simply to stick to a price and clarify that the opportunity is *now.* "If you walk away from this deal, the item will be gone or the price will increase."

The negotiation should begin in a more fact-finding, relationship-building mode. Once a relationship has been established and both parties feel comfortable in dialogue, questions regarding the desire of the product or service need to be asked. If you are selling a product or service, generally, the other party will either state why they need the product or service, or conversely will state why you should sell the goods to them. By listening to the arguments presented, not only does your party become more informed, but a path toward decision making is forged.

North Americans tend to want the "quick sale." Thinking and delaying is unnerving. However, delays can be beneficial for you if you have patience and properly time your pounce. There are other areas that should be discussed to understand the full value of the deal. Ask pertinent questions that lead the buyer into describing the value of your product. Who else has these products or services? What other benefits are there? What guarantees come with the deal? What type of follow-up support will be received?

Once all questions are answered and time has been spent in the negotiation process, the pounce can be conducted. Once considerable conversations have occurred, the other party knows they have time invested in the negotiation. They are interested in your product or service and have spent much time understanding the value and benefits, now they want a price they can be comfortable with so they can move forward to realize the benefits. To lose the deal means loss of time spent, which equals a loss of revenue.

At this point, a quick statement should be made as to a benefit of doing business with you that go beyond just the mere money transaction. Here are some examples:

- "I have other contacts that could benefit from your business. I would like to put you in touch with them."
- "If I were to sell this item to you, it could be good advertisement for you."
- "You will be the first one in your market to have this capability."

One statement should be made, followed by silence. At this moment, the typical North American will often not be able to hold his mouth closed through the silence. They will fold and try and discuss other reasons for buying or selling at this moment in time. If both parties can come to an agreement on price, you have a deal. If objections still come, asking clarifying questions is considered a nonaggressive request for close. A simple comment like this is in order: "Well, we all agree that there is a tremendous amount of value offered here. Are we making a price decision or a value consideration?"

With this, the pounce has been sprung, and the deal must close quickly. The other party can request financing arrangements, reduced pricing, or additional benefits at no extra cost; however, now you are in the driver's seat. You can state the price you need to make the sale work. With the other party reeling, an agreement will be made or it will be time to move on. Regardless, the pounce has been completed and most often, you will reap the rewards.

European

The European is the ancestry of the North American. The foundation of the North American resides here; however, negotiation has changed since the colonies were formed. Europeans have learned that the deal can wait. Family values, vacation, and general quality of life have found the way to the top of the values list. Clean air and water, recycling, and public transportation have become higher priorities in daily life. Dealing with these values, one must ensure that they are not compromised. Many Europeans have six weeks minimum vacation every year and are encouraged to take it all with the family. Men often receive paternity leave to help with the formative months of child rearing. For some, sabbaticals are conducted from the job every five to seven years.

In this type of society, Europeans can wait for a deal. It will often be suggested by a European that "The deal sounds good; however, let's wait until after my sabbatical."

Most deals do not hinge on price. Instead, they are based more on relationships and trust. In order to gain this trust, you need to be concerned for the other party, prepare for a long sales cycle, and ask what is important to the customer. The value proposition must be based around what the customer states. Much like the North American, a salesperson must ask questions about the customer and find what is important to him or her. Once the value of the product has been established, a desire to close the deal must be created. This desire can be created through leading discussion with questions and statements like the following:

- "What happens if we wait until after your sabbatical? Can you still take full advantage of this product?"
- "If you obtain the product now, your company can familiarize and utilize it, so upon your return, all will flow seamlessly."

Continue to probe to find the reason to conduct the deal sooner rather than later. If you push too hard, you might harm the relationship as well as the deal. One must always be cognizant of the relationship. However, if you can convey a value to the purchase and a reason to complete the transaction sooner than later, then you have your pounce setup. Summarizing the reason to purchase now should solidify the need. Often, the European will refrain from a quick decision, which is not the norm for business deal. However, if you created the need and timeliness, the likelihood of closing within days rather than weeks or months increases.

Asian

Asian culture is far different from Western culture, and negotiations are as far apart as are the cultures. Much of the Orient is raised to believe that bartering and haggling are common ways of doing business. A deal is never made on the first price asked. In the Orient, it is customary to earn the deal. If you pay too much, you did not earn the lower price. Conversely, if you obtain a great price for a product, you earned the deal by being a good negotiator.

Much of this historical culture has changed with wealth. Japan, South Korea, Hong Kong, and the new China have achieved immense wealth over the past three decades. With wealth, there is less bartering or bargaining. Value is viewed much higher than price when one has affluence. However, negotiation is ingrained in the heritage. Less wealthy countries, such as Vietnam, Cambodia, Thailand, and highly populated countries, such as India and most of China, still rely heavily on bargaining for everything from toothpaste to automobiles.

In the Asian culture, another key ingredient to negotiation is silence. This is a concept foreign to many in Western civilization. The gift of gab plays against the Oriental trader. It is within silence where the pounce lies. Often Western and Eastern cultures will go to the bargaining table and attempt to negotiate. Far too often, the negotiations are between only the Western people discussing how to cut price or increase service.

Silence can be unnerving to many in Western civilization. Raised in a culture where talking a good talk shows one's confidence and exudes knowledge is considered commonplace in the society. In the Asian society, it is quite the opposite. Due to this, North Americans and Europeans often come off as shoddy and brash business folk out to make a quick buck. In many negotiations, the Westerner will submit a price for goods or services. The Asian businessperson will carefully consider the offer and "mull it over" for a while before even asking the first question. This unnerves and sometimes infuriates the Westerner. Asians have no problems looking over a negotiation and remaining quiet for thirty to sixty minutes—or even days—depending on the complexity of the deal. That is a lengthy time to sit and remain quiet. Often, the Westerner will assume the deal is insufficient or unsatisfactory in some way. At this time, the Westerner will discuss other ways to make the deal sweeter, by either lowering the price "for today only," or perhaps offering more services or support.

This is where the Asian already has conducted the pounce. Once the Westerner is reeling from the silence, left to his or her own devices, the price will come down and the product will increase in scope all by itself. The pounce is actually in the silence rather than finding a value proposition to hone in on.

Conversely, if you can tolerate the lengthy silent moments and endure through, then in effect, you have sprung the pounce. For silence is a moment to ponder and think about all the reasons to conduct the deal. When one talks through the thinking time, it only harms the initial negotiation. When Asian negotiators are silent, it means that you have given them a viable solution and price. You have already made the pounce, and they are thinking of questions or possibly one discussion on lower price. However, you are close and should not blow the deal rattling off with your mouth.

The pounce does not necessarily mean conversation or quick talking needs to be employed. Often the best pounce is in silence.

Middle Eastern

The Middle Eastern culture is not much different from the Asian culture in that the people are born and raised on haggling. Haggling for groceries is as common as haggling for finished goods and services. Nothing is purchased for asking price or label price. In these cultures, relationship sales are important; however, even more important is how you treat the customer. Showing respect for the others involved in the negotiation is paramount. Crossing your legs and showing the soles of your shoes or talking over others while trying to conduct business, all before getting to know the individual, are all considered rude behaviors. In the Middle East, respect is the supreme gesture or character quality, and it should not be compromised by acting superior. If you come across as arrogant or rude, you will be dismissed quickly.

In cultures where one is inexperienced, mimicking others is perhaps the best way to blend in and not degrade the others. Pay particular attention to the way people sit and react to others in the room. In the Middle Eastern culture, usually the older statesman will be considered the wiser, more knowledgeable negotiator. Others will look to this person to ensure the deal is being conducted accordingly. This is where the pounce begins. Once you understand the dynamics, once you get into a groove with the body language and cultural offerings, then you can talk business and peddle your products. To pounce before you have established this rapport would be considered negotiation suicide. Often negotiations will transpire over drinks or meals. During these times, trust is established and respect is given. The pounce can be easily made during these more personable times, rather than at the negotiating table. Remaining respectful to those who lead the meeting, never swaying from utmost respect, and always creating a positive atmosphere—this is the pounce. If you've passed the test, by the end of the evening, you will receive your reward.

Latin

The Latin culture, much like their founding fathers from Europe, is one that has close ties with family. Family bonds are stronger than any other and therefore must never be compromised by any negotiation. Similar to the European culture, family is the utmost important priority in life, and everything after that can take time to set up. In the Latin culture, deals do not have to be conducted quickly; however, unlike Europeans, the culture is not adverse to a quick deal either. Latinos are used to haggling for items, but they often choose not to. In many stores, prices are fixed and are not subject to negotiation. In other stores, prices are not clearly marked and the offered price is often many times higher than the actual price needed to close the deal.

A combination of North American and European influence lies within the Latin culture. A tactful approach with a concern for family and personal well-being combined with a value proposition may work best. In other words, asking what the product or service can do for the customer is a good start, but then asking what it will mean to his or her family and friends allows them to think of the important reasons for conducting the deal. "Wouldn't your wife and children enjoy seeing you more often because you purchased a product like this? Freeing up your time and getting the job done seems to be the best of both worlds." Value statements like this will give you a pounce statement that should not insult or turn away any customer. Listen to the objections, if any, and continue to hone in on the value to the customer and family.

Third World

Third world negotiations are similar to negotiations discussed for the Latin culture. This is not saying that the Latin nations are all third world countries. It is merely a statement relaying the fact that third world nation often have strong family ties. In countries that do not have fortunes to spend or surpluses to extract from and have high unemployment and low wage jobs for the majority of workers, spending and negotiations are low on the priority list. Most spending is done on mere essentials and nothing more. If a company is interested in procuring a product or service, it most likely feels that it needs the specific product or service and cannot function without. In these types of situations, negotiation is a requirement, and thus the seller has a leg up in many ways. With competition in the world driving down prices, a third world customer will seek many quotes and sources of services before buying. There are only two ways to win this negotiation: the best price over anyone else, or the best relationship and support.

How do you demonstrate the best service and support? Again, relationship building is key. Ask the customer why they need your product or service. Continue to ask questions as to what they would like to gain out of the negotiation. Often the customer merely wants pricing that is within reason on a product that will complete the task requested. Generally quality and reliability are not the largest issues; focus is more on will the product meet the needs of today. Third world countries often cannot see well into the future, because the future can change quickly. A strong sense of what works now for a good price is key. Drive the negotiation along these lines. When the customer agrees, begin demonstrating how your product or service will suffice and complete the task at hand. This is your pounce. Concentrating on uncertain futures and the requirement now can solidify the deal quicker.

Some feel this tactic is praying on the weaker economies and taking advantage of an unfortunate or urgent situation. This is not so. The fact is that if a company or person is looking for a deal, they clearly need a product or service. How that product or service is conveyed is usually the largest difference. Why not sell your product rather than having your competition sell theirs? Don't be afraid to pounce, regardless of the situation. The pounce is merely taking the time to ensure the negotiation favors your services and your value propositions.

Here is a quick reference list of the time to pounce for various negotiations around the world.

Region	Set-up for Pounce	Pounce time
North American	Ask for the value of the product. Why is the other party interested?	Restate the value to the customer, and state the reason to close soon.
European	Ask for the value of the product, and ask what would happen if you waited to close the deal.	Restate the value to the customer, and suggest positive scenarios to close sooner than later.
Asian	Present your products and services to the fullest.	Remain silent and respectful until questions are asked.
Middle Eastern	Earn respect and mimic behavior patterns. Earn the relationship.	When asked about the deal, respectfully educate and remain silent for questions.
Latin	Begin with relationship building and then ask about interest.	Once the other is interested in doing business with you, continue to talk value.
Third World	Probe about future concerns and then present product and services to the fullest.	Listen for questions; however, always refer to the fix now and the uncertain future.

Again, every person is different, and not all cultures fit into a simple table. Every negotiation needs to be treated with care and understanding. However, this table gives a snapshot into various regions of the world and what often works in those regional negotiations.

Looking for Work

For the majority of our working lives, we are making employment decisions in some manner or other. If you are in a management position, you will need to make decisions on hiring to grow your organization and to fend off attrition in your workgroup. But most workers have employment concerns dealing with the flip-side of the table—interviewing for a job. Whether you are employed or not, looking for the right job is only half the battle. Interviewing correctly and pouncing at the right time can lead to not only a successful interview and job offer, but a promotional path for your career.

The next three sections discuss various situations surrounding finding employees or employers. The recruiting section is first so the reader can understand what and how a recruiter should think. By understanding your interviewer, you may be able to see their side and talk to their concerns better.

Recruiting

In real estate, the top three elements of finding a good property are location, location, location. Similarly, with any successful organization, the top three priorities need to be recruiting, recruiting, and recruiting. These were the top three priorities of arguably the greatest coach of all times, Coach John Wooden of UCLA basketball fame. John Wooden, a great philosopher, always knew that coaching, mentoring, and guiding were key elements to having a successful team, but at the core was achieving a great recruiting effort for the team.

Some managers get complacent once they have a fully staffed team. This is a fundamental flaw that most employers make, feeling that recruiting when you cannot hire is a waste of time. In fact, it is the best effort you can make toward keeping your team active and on their toes. Seeing new potential recruits on a consistent basis does two things for your team. One, it creates an atmosphere where low performers know that they need to perform to at least minimal levels or they may be replaced. Two, continually recruiting when you have a full team lets you tell the world that you have a class act team that takes only the best. Whatever industry you are in, word gets around that your team takes only the best and has a pipeline of candidates if needed; when that happens, your value as a manager and the team's value in the organization and the industry increase tremendously.

When recruiting, the pounce is key to finding quality recruits versus job jumpers or desperate job seekers. There are a number of ways to find candidates for jobs you may be looking to fill, even for in the future, if you don't have positions to fill immediately. The most common method nowadays is Internet recruiting. Sites like Monster.com, CareerBuilder.com, and dozens of others are easy to use to scan, filter, and sort for various parameters to filter for resumes you think may be a match for what you are looking for. One you have narrowed the field to qualified candidates, it is the time to pounce. Ask the candidate when they would like to meet. The answer to that question alone speaks volumes. If the candidate says "anytime" or if they can see you during normal working hours, it tells you they either don't have a job currently, or perhaps they just don't care about the one they have. Contract workers often need normal working business hours to work on obligations they are contracted for. If the candidate has "plenty of time," this may be a sign of a desperate candidate and one who may have some hidden issues. If the candidate wants to meet after hours or at lunch, it lets you know that they most likely have a job and they carefully manage their time. In this case, the candidate initiates the pounce.

Another method of recruiting is to go to job fairs or recruiting events. These fairs are full of candidates, many not a match for what you are looking for. Should you get a booth at one of these events, you are subjected to hundreds of candidates tossing their resumes at you, hoping their resume sticks with some company. You get to sift through the hundreds, hope you can remember a few, and call the select few who intrigued you for a fleeting moment. The better method is to be more proactive. Work the floor—don't be a part of it. During the off-peak hours, sit at your booth and take the resumes; but be aware that from 11:30 a.m. until 1:30 p.m. are the peak hours for the lunch crowd. Here come the candidates who have jobs and probably are looking to change for the better versus change out of necessity. Walk the floor during these hours and check out the candidates. Linger around the lines, eavesdrop on conversations and job dialogues. Look and listen for candidates who look, act, and talk the part that you are looking to fill. When you find a candidate whom you are interested in, slip them your business card and have a brief conversation. Make sure they are aware that you run a top-notch team and are interested in a few good candidates to fill a position desired by many. Make the pounce quick and effective. You should see many more qualified candidates either calling you later that week or coming to your booth immediately to get more information about your company. Pounce right and you make the desirable candidates come to you versus waiting for that knight in shining armor.

When Employed

Remember the rules of recruiting and apply them to your daily efforts in looking for a job. Remember that employers do not want to see a desperate job seeker who will take anything that comes his or her way. If you have a job, no matter how much you may want to get out of it, you still have a job. Utilize your situation to make sure you get the right job next time.

When employed, not only do you not want to inconvenience your current job by interviewing during peak hours, you also do not want to compromise your current job by becoming seen as a potential "flight risk," which could get you terminated. Never burn bridges. Make sure that when you leave your job, your employer will miss your absence. Minimally, your current employer should have no ill words to say about your work ethics.

Even if you feel your current employer deems you of little importance, when you work hard through the last day, they will remember the dedicated worker you were, and regret you leaving soon after you are gone. When you leave in a bad way, either suddenly or with malice, you leave with the past employer never giving you a reference—but worse, glad that you are gone.

Keeping in mind that you want to leave on good terms actually sets you up better for the pounce. Your future employer sees that you are dedicated, creating a challenge to get you over to their company. I have often seen individuals who have gone to their future employers and asked for more time or tried to clarify what they will receive at the new job, because their current employer is working hard to keep them. When a future employer sees a fight to keep you at your old job, it speaks volumes about you and the regard your past employer has for you. This sets you up with a reputation of a good employee even before the first day of your new job.

Everyone likes a challenge, though not an impossible one. If your current employer wants to keep you and incentivizes you to stay, make sure the future employer knows this. However, be careful not to cross a line where you lose a great job opportunity because you negotiated too much or asked for too much. At the same time, when you have a present job, you are in the driver's seat and can ask for more out of the position, since even in the worst case, you're still employed.

There are questions you can ask that show you have career goals and broader concerns other than just compensation. Employers want to be asked about the path that will be laid out rather than just "What's in it for me?" type of questions. Here is where the pounce lies. During the interview process, ask questions like:

- "What is the timeline in which you are looking to fill your vacancy?"
- "What would you think about creating a slightly different position?"
- "What is / are the career path(s) for me at your firm?"

- "What premiums do you offer for someone like me who is already employed and may need an extra incentive to come over to your company?"
- "What types of individuals seem to excel at your firm?"
- "Could you describe for me your typical management style and the type of employee who works well within you company?"
- "Where are your major concerns that need to be immediately addressed in this assignment?"
- "What is your policy on providing product and industry training so employees can further develop their skills?"
- "How will my performance be measured? By whom?"
- "Are there any weaknesses in the program that you are working on improving?"
- "Can you give me an idea of the expansion plans for your company in the next twelve months?"
- "Are there any new products or programs that will become available in the near future that will help to make your company more competitive?"

Once these questions are answered, you can ask for incentives or premiums for certain goals achieved. If the interviewer is taken aback by your question, remember the power of silence. The first person to speak typically loses. Let them say they offer no premiums or incentives. If they do offer, now you pounce and ask if you are eligible, and if so, what will it take to get the process started. Now you have gone for the close. If the interviewer states that no incentives are offered, you need to ask what they would do when they see a candidate whom they would really like to hire. Whatever the answer is, the next question should be "Do I fit in that category?"

If you do, you need to remind your future employer that finding good, qualified candidates is expensive, and training, teaching, and retaining is even more expensive. You need to emphasize that you are at your current position because you are good at your job, and rewarding you to come over would be less expensive than to keep looking for another candidate who comes close to your abilities. If you feel like you are pushing too much, remember, this is the time to see if the new potential employer is worth coming over to or if they are the same as what you are leaving. Also remember, incentives do not need to be monetary. Ask for extra vacation time, ask for earlier arrival or departure hours. Usually, the extra vacation time can work.

Whatever extra incentive or perk you ask for, make sure you preface why you are asking. For example, you may say "I believe in giving my company my all. I also believe it's important to take breaks periodically to ensure employees stay fresh with ideas and are consistently rejuvenated. One extra week of vacation may not truly cost the company money, as it may bring in much more growth potential from satisfied employees working harder when at work. For this reason, I would like to have an extra week of vacation than your average starting employee."

The pounce can be for benefits, extra vacation, extra pay, or many other items. Once you get on these subjects, it is almost implied that you have the job—you are now negotiating for the details. Pounce complete. Now you just ask for the starting date and the offer letter.

When Unemployed

When unemployed, you may feel that you are not in a power position to pounce. As soon as you feel deflated or powerless, your confidence erodes. A loss of confidence exudes from people and appears in the form of desperation. This is a trap you cannot afford to fall into. When the right position is available, you can and must pounce on the opportunity at the right time. Remember what you learned in the pounce time when you are employed; the same rules apply when you are unemployed. Do not go to interviews whenever the interviewers suggest scheduling them; instead, request lunchtime or after-hour interviews. Merely requesting this separates you from the rest of the candidate pool who succumb to any time granted by the interviewer. If the subject comes up that you should have time since you are unemployed, you must come across as someone with many options. Explain that peak daytime hours are not conducive to conducting your business nor is it the opportune time for the company that is conducting the interview. By creating a time when other distractions are minimized, the interview can be much more focused and participants can be more attentive. Interviews conducted during normal peak working hours tend to have many disruptions. The impression of the interview is often confusing, and both parties don't know where they stand. Usually employers consider this a weak interview and will look toward other candidates who made their presence felt. By mentioning these points in a positive manner to your interviewer, you will already start off on an impressive note.

Now for the unemployment cover. No one likes to hear that you have been let go from your previous job for nonperformance. Even worse is to hear a potential candidate spout off about how bad their previous job was and how bad management ran the operations. This creates a cloud over the interview, and usually no one wants to hire a complainer. Most often, the feeling is that if a candidate did not like his or her past employer, there is a good chance they may not work out here. Remember, always discuss the positives and let the interviewer know that you are no longer employed due to a mutual reason. That reason could be a downsizing in the company. The reason could be that you wanted to work in an environment that better suited your talents and created a better, more motivating climate for you to flourish in. These are all reasons that leave a positive note as to why you are unemployed, yet these reasons show ambition—enough to show you want to pick the right job for you, and not just the first one that comes along.

It is important that the interviewer feels that you are *selecting* your next place of employment and that if you see the right company, that company will benefit. This is the time when you need to talk about your track record of success at other companies you have worked at.

Before you start the interview process, *you should prepare a few answers to common questions asked*, so you sound put together and intelligent. Here are a few questions that are often asked during an interview:

- "What was or were the greatest accomplishments you had at your previous employment?"
- "What are your best and worst attributes?"
- "What can you do for our company?"

Other questions will arise, but these three are usually asked and often stump many interviewees. Make sure that before any interview, you do two things: First, research the company and find aspects of the firm that interest you or are positive notes on the company. Bringing these items to the forefront tells the interviewer that you have done your homework and are not just winging the interview. The second thing you need to do is be prepared with answers to the above-mentioned questions. If you are not prepared for the interview, you demonstrate that you will not be prepared for the job at stake. It doesn't take very long to prepare answers to these questions, but it does take some thought. Only you know the best answers to these questions.

Whatever answers you do come up with should be answers that you are proud of. When it comes to your worst attributes, never lay out attributes that are considered good to have, yet you are poor at; instead, state that your worst attributes are attributes that can be considered good to be bad at, and make sure you have examples of these so you do not sound trite in your answers. For example, a trait that you could be "weak" at is that sometimes you pay too much attention to detail. Then come up with an example in which it was an issue, but not a big issue. Here is an example:

"My weakest attribute would be my enthusiastic attention to detail. While that might sound like a good thing, at times it can cause extra questioning in group discussions and can delay deadlines due to issues discovered. Like the time when we ..."

You can emphasize that you are organized and pay attention to detail, but you may be considered a perfectionist and need to work on letting go when tasks get to a certain point. However, if you are not an organized person, do not use this "weak" attribute. There are many to choose from. You could profess to being too involved with time management. Or maybe you are too much of a pleaser, and while you know team atmosphere is beneficial, you tend to take on too much to ensure everyone is taken care of. You can be overcommunicative; it sure beats keeping everything inside, but perhaps it can get you in a bind at times. You may want to say you are too competitive. In a sales environment, that can be considered very attractive; but again, it does have its downsides, like making others feel inept and not a part of the team.

These are all attributes that, although they have their downfalls, have tremendous upside—and if that's your weakest attribute, employers will love you. These are the answers that you must be prepared with to start your pounce.

Now that you have answered the interviewer's questions as well as asked questions about the firm based on research you have done, now is the time for the pounce. The interviewer should have seen by now that you have your act together; you listen and ask and answer the right questions in the right way. Now you need to ask for the next steps in the process:

- "What is your full interview process?"
- "Are you the final decision point in this process?"
- "When will you be making a decision to hire your best candidate?"

These questions set you up for the close. Depending on the answers, you need to let the interviewer know that your time—and their time—is precious. Let them know that you would like to move through the process as quickly as possible, since you do have other options on the table. This allows the interviewer(s) to know that they need to act on you quickly and possibly prioritize you over other candidates. It may lead to a sign-on bonus to ensure retention of your employment. You may even want to ask about other benefits that may sway your decision, such as vacation time, sign-on bonuses, or other perks that the company has to offer. This shows that you are aggressive and *not* desperate. A desperate candidate rarely gets the job.

This is your pounce. This is where you not only can cinch the deal, but also get a better-negotiated salary, sign-on bonus, vacation time, or other benefits you may desire. What it absolutely does is separate you from any other candidate who put themselves in the weaker position of letting the interviewer drive the interview all the way from start to finish. Though that may sound good for the interviewer, lackadaisical interviews show no strength in character and no strong passion to move forward and get the job going, in contrast to what you just demonstrated.

School Studies

School studies are different from most other pounce circumstances. Playing the pounce game in school is much like tipping for service; one should always tip well in the beginning of a relationship, not at the end when all is said and done. When you go to a hotel, tip well in the very beginning. All service personnel will swoon over you for the rest of your stay. If you reserve your tipping for the end of your stay, you will get average service throughout your stay and will only be well thought of after you leave. Get the biggest bang for your buck up front.

School is much the same as the tipping example. Study hard up front, get good grades, and you will get on the teacher's good side. Teachers and professors get biases quickly. They sum up students within the first few weeks of every school year, trying to figure out who needs more help and who are the strong students who need less help. Those that need more help will get more attention; however, those students will be watched and graded more severely. The strong student will be praised and soon be considered A level, requiring little help. As the school year progresses, teachers and professors undergo more time constraints. Grading numerous and more complex papers becomes more of a burden. At these times, teachers and professors will begin to glance at papers and make grading decisions based on a few passages or problems. Most of the grading will come from reputation. Those students with strong reputations will quite often be passed over and get the A reports. The students who have struggled more concerning material understanding will undergo more scrutiny and most likely, receive lesser grades.

Many B and C students study just as hard as the A students, yet receive lesser grades. B and C students need to submit the same papers, take the same tests and quizzes, and attend the classes just like the A students. Society tends to think that A students are more intelligent. Excuses like "I'm just not a good student" or "I'm not that smart in this subject" are quite often heard when students get labeled as average or below-average students. I am a firm believer that most of us are of similar intelligence. Grades, judgment, and other forms of praise, including raises at work and reputations of all sorts, are earned from judgments made early on in the relationships formed. Intelligence has very little to do with reputations.

For this reason, should you choose to work hard for your grades, why not work hard in the beginning and less toward the end. The end of the school year is usually in the summer, when everyone, including teachers and professors, become more lenient. Even if the semester ends in winter, Christmas grades are often more lenient as well.

So why put more effort into your schoolwork in the beginning? The key to successful grades is to study hard for the first three to four weeks. However, good study habits are only a small piece of the grade equation. Get to know your teacher or professor. A personal touch will go a long way. It is much more difficult to grade harshly when you really like someone. This does not mean you become the teacher's pet; however, hanging around after class a few minutes, say every three out of five class times, can go a long way throughout the year. Get to know your teacher or professor. Understand what they want to see throughout the school term. Often times, these after-class meetings will result in the teacher or professor explaining exactly what their expectations are. Once you know those, writing papers for them or solving problems for them will be far easier, because you will know how to wordsmith your essays or show your math work.

Usually, after a few weeks of special attention shown to the teacher or professor, you can slowly reduce the number of after-class visitations and the length of visitations. Teachers and professors will get busier and have less time to socialize and divulge tidbits of information that can help you throughout the year. By this point in time, they have already established reputations on most individuals. By now, you should know yours. Unless you dramatically change your behavior or your work performed, it should be smooth sailing from this point forward. You should be relatively certain of what your grades will be. At this point, an occasional visit is good practice, just as turning in your homework on time and doing your best on reports and tests. However, the frequency of visits can be reduced considerably as can the intense work levels.

So the good old "study hard and do the best you can" philosophy will always hold true, but maximizing your efforts is even more key to obtaining good grades and becoming a more well-rounded individual. Most students who do well in school and athletics and even carry on with part-time jobs and what-not, often are not smarter, but wiser. These students know when to pounce on the teachers and get the reputations that will carry them throughout the school year. Learn from these individuals—strike fast and get your good reputation early. Pounce in the first three to four weeks of the school term.

When to Study

School studies are often difficult, no matter what time of day or night. So how do you study diligently while taking six classes, holding down a job, and having chores to take care of as well? The key is to pounce on the studies at the height of your energy level.

Jobs require a certain set amount of work. Usually, while in school, students don't have the most difficult, brain-taxing jobs. If you think you do, wait until you graduate. Most jobs can be done after your dinner and after your studies are completed. Chores will always be around and should be done, for the most part, when you are winding down the day. Complete the chores and go to bed knowing that all has been done. This gives you better rest as well. So when should you study?

Studies should be completed before dinner and before your body begins its digestive process. Eat a small snack before studying. Get your energy source so you can sustain your energy for the duration of your homework or study time. However, do not eat a large meal before studying or completing homework. Consuming a large amount of food does two bad things to your head: One, your body begins its digestive process, thus slowing down your brain waves, making you drowsy. The digestive process will require more blood to circulate in the stomach region, not to the head, where the blood is needed for thought. Two, your normal routine is most likely not to eat a large lunch before your intense school requirements. Eating large amounts of food before you do your homework or study will get your body and mind out of that mode of operation. Eat light and study hard. You should find this the most effective way to ensure minimal studying yet the maximum results. Eat dinner after your homework or studies and then work or play as desired. Make sure you get the rest you need, and remember to pounce on the homework as soon as you get home.

Tips for the Teach

Now knowing when the smart students study, teachers or professors should be astute to these tricks. How to combat this is a trick in itself. To combat the emotional aspect of getting to know your students and forming an opinion and possibly being swayed to be more lenient to some, as a teacher, you want to make teaching more consistent. The natural tendency for many is to blurt out everything you can to students right away. You are so excited about all you know and about sharing it with the class that most lectures start out at a fast pace, slow down in the middle, and then ratchet up a notch or two for the finals. This burns out many students as well as teachers.

If anything deters from being consistent, try to do negative splits. "Negative splits" is a running term. When running long distances like during a marathon, the true marathoner strives to run negative splits meaning that the runner completes the second half of the marathon faster than the first half. The purpose of this is that you finish strong and have quicker recuperation time after the race.

The same can be applied to teaching a course. If you blast the class with all your knowledge up front and set up numerous tests and quizzes right away, you burn out students and yourself, grading until the wee hours and stressing that students are not getting what you are teaching. Instead, you should create a curriculum whereby the first half of the semester or quarter is consistent with tests or quizzes every week or two, and then start ratcheting up the tests either in timing or in difficulty. This gets students to get interest in the course and then ramp up their efforts. Likewise, as the teacher, you will see staged improvements in each student as they increase their efforts. You will grade the most difficult, lengthy, and time consuming test at the conclusion of the class instead of early on. This allows recuperation time early in the next semester or quarter and a much more restful and thought-provoking next term.

The pounce is set for the end of the term and not the beginning. Show patience with your teaching and with your students. You will keep more students from withdrawing, you will keep more students interested, and you will keep your sanity throughout the term. The pounce is saved to allow for a ramping up of knowledge until the final exam.

Personal Relationships

In relationships and negotiations of a more personal nature, emotions get in the way more than with business dealings. In most business dealings, if all goes awry, you can always leave. You make your move and pounce on the opportunity. The worst thing that can happen in a business relationship is the parties break up and go their separate ways. This may mean getting a new job or starting another venture.

However, with personal relationships, there are more feelings involved and more vulnerabilities exposed, which make matters more difficult if things get tough. The key to dealing with others regarding personal matters is not to try to not make things personal.

When frustrations set in, many have a tendency to start shooting barbs at the other person. They may bring up past experiences or dealings that were not handled well by the other person. These are rudimentary tools used to show dominance, superiority, or righteousness. It also shows that the other was *wrong*. Whenever you state to someone directly or indirectly that they are wrong, the conversation usually does not go well after that.

The best advice is to stay away from these kinds of conversations. If you feel the conversation is heading down the path where one is trying to be righteous and make the other wrong, get out immediately and set a time to reconvene. Getting out without a specific time to reconvene implies that you are running away from criticism or running away from tough conversation. Never say "we'll talk about this later" and leave. Instead, make a simple request to reconvene the conversation at a better time for both parties involved. "My head is not as clear as I'd like it to be for me to give the proper attention to your concerns. Can we continue this conversation tomorrow after lunch?" You are actually setting yourself up for a pounce in the future. By setting a time to come back and discuss more rationally, you become the dominant figure, setting the tone and the pace for the discussion.

When negotiating on a personal level, the key is to make the other feel right about the decisions that are made. If everyone feels they get what they want, all parties come together and go forward. Here is where the pounce lies. Find out what each person in the negotiation desires. What outcome are they hoping for, or what motivates them? There is no better way to discover this information than to just ask.

When you ask others what they want, if the desired outcome is far-fetched, it may become obvious to them as they are stating their desires. Often, when you put in words what you desire, the desire seems quite contrite and simple. Let the others state what they want and let them negotiate down for you. As with foreign business dealings, the first to speak usually loses. Ask what the desired outcome should be, and listen. Usually the other will go down a path and then start relinquishing items that are nonessential or nonimportant. Once they make their desires known, now you have the leverage and the power. You have just asked for their desires, yet not given yours up. Now you can spin your desires to come close to theirs, while getting exactly what you want.

The main point is to have the others state what they want to hear from you. Now you are in the position to negotiate what you want, yet show the other that they will get what they want. The pounce is simply in the first question that should be asked and quite often is not asked: "What do you want to get out of this?" Asking a question along these lines as soon as you see a negotiation coming will take you a long way and usually get you exactly what you want.

Finding Your Mate

Ah, love is in the air! We've heard that many times in our lives, especially when we are young and every pretty girl or handsome boy who walks by and looks at us gives us butterflies. Lust is one thing, and the pounce is more overt. Romance is an entirely different desire. Romance stems from lust, but then it progresses into a relationship blossoming from the mutual desire of the two individuals. The definition of "romance" depends on the individuals. For some, romance is sitting in front of the TV and watching a favorite show together. For others, it's enjoying a fine wine over a nice meal followed by a walk on the beach. Romance can be just being together for a period of time to talk and share ideas. Whatever your interpretation of romance is, make sure it's close to the same for both parties involved. If one feels that romance is lavishing each other with gifts and fine dinning, and the other feels romance is going to a ball game together, there better be some heart-to-heart dialogue before that relationship gets too involved and expectations are not properly set.

The Supremes sang the song "You Can't Hurry Love." Although that sentiment is true in theory, you can enhance your opportunities. With the right pounce, indeed, you can hurry it along quite a bit. In today's society, we have more options to search for compatible romantic relationships than ever before. Previously, a setup from a friend, a meeting at a party, or the cliché meeting at a bar were the most common ways to meet the potential candidate for a relationship and possible marriage down the line. Today, we have the Internet. With the introduction of social-networking sites, it has become common to surf personal ads, chat online with a large group, and sign up for a dating or mate-matching service. With literally thousands of mates to choose from, the task of finding a person to relate to has gone to pairing down your options to find the best fit for your personality. There are also more avenues to join shared-interest clubs, such as bicycling clubs, gaming clubs, outdoor adventure clubs, etc.

By the time you hit your midtwenties, through school, friends, clubs, online matching sites, parties, bars, hangout spots, and other means of meeting people, you will have the possibility of meeting not dozens, but thousands of potential mates. Unfortunately, you can't pounce on every opportunity. We don't have time to court, date, and get to really know thousands of potential mates before getting to settle down with "the one." How do we go about getting the right one? Marriage will be discussed later, but for now, just finding the one to have a relationship with is tough enough.

Most online dating services have lengthy questionnaires asking detailed questions about what you would like in a relationship. While some ask the usual questions, such as "What are your interests and hobbies?", many are now asking for more details to narrow your search to create very specific matches.

The problems with these questionnaires are two-fold: One, the person answering the questions often does not know what he or she truly wants. They may feel that fine dining and walks on the beach are the ideal things to say they want in life, but when it gets down to it, they may not really enjoy those activities all that much—especially not every night. The second issue is that opposites attract, and often we do not want to have a relationship with our mirror image. We say we want someone who wants the same things as us, but then we find out that we do not grow personally with an individual exactly like us. Spontaneity, differences in opinion, desire for alternative options from daily activities are great attributes to have with another person. So how does all this correlate to finding that "one" person and pouncing?

If you answer the questionnaires to meet an exact person, you will likely find that person. Be careful what you ask for. The beauty of the old-school method of meeting others was that you got what was available at the particular party, bar, or friend's group. It forced you to see different people with points of view. With the online services, you may answer questions so specifically or place an ad so pointed that you will only get the person you are specifically asking for—usually, a spitting image of yourself.

Instead, it is better to place ads that are generic in nature, yet inviting and witty. Ask your friends to help you write the narrative about you. Look through other ads to see how they are written, but don't just copy the ones that you like. Write yours in a way that would attract others who are *not* exactly like you. Do not be deceiving, but show that you are open to possibilities. Don't just answer questions the way you would want others to answer. Answer the questions in an open-ended manner or in as rounded a way as possible. Obviously, you will want to weed out some individuals who do not share those elements that are truly important to you. If religion is important to you, don't write that you don't care about religion. But aside from the important issues, let loose.

The best option for finding potential matches may be at social interest club for activities that you really enjoy. At these clubs, common ground is a certainty, in that you will meet people who at the very least have a good interest in pursuing the same activities you are interested in becoming more familiar with. You might find more commonalities with someone in a social interest club, but there are many more attributes to people than just an activity interest. Get to know the members, and discover the other dimensions of their personalities.

The pounce will not take place when meeting your mirror image. In that situation, there will usually be a natural attraction with no pounce necessary, and then later that relationship will fall apart. The pounce should be reserved for the catch that is out there that might go away if not acted on. When you meet that special someone, you'll know it in your heart. Quite often, the match may not seem logical. When you meet that one who gives you butterflies, the one who irks you in ways that you couldn't imagine, the one who drives you nuts yet you can't get out of your head—when that person comes along, you need to pounce.

There are times in life where we are shy, introverted, or just plain and simply not confident in ourselves. But when we want something so badly that we can't imagine living without it, we gain strength that can be superhuman. If you are starving or dehydrated and you see food or water, nothing will stop you from eating or drinking. Likewise, if you do not have companionship, you need to pounce—not at anything that moves, but for the one who makes your world spin around. At this particular time in life, you have to reach deep inside and go for it. If he or she is not interested, there will be others; but you must try if this person is the one you feel could change your life in a way you really want.

The pounce must come in a way that will be direct, noticeable, and unique. You must set a time, a place, and a manner in which you make your intentions clear. At the same time, just asking to get together for dinner and movie may come off as mundane and not worthy of taking you up on your offer. Surprise the other with tickets to the concert that he or she has wanted to go to, or ask for a date to a particular show that the other has expressed interest in. Perhaps a hot air balloon ride for breakfast or a night out at the go-kart track. Whatever you decide to offer as a date, make sure it's something special, unusual, and most importantly, something that the other really wants to partake in.

Nothing is more important than letting the other know that you have listened and heard what they have said. Show interest in an activity they discussed or described, and you will be looked at in an entirely different light. Find out what the person volunteers for, does in their spare time, or just wishes they could try once. Set that event up, and you're done. The pounce is mostly complete. Once at the event, you will feel the moment. There will be a time when the other person will look at you, thank you for taking them, or just smile beamingly. At that moment, you just smile back and say, "I thought you'd like this. I would like to do more things that excite you—that thrill you like this."

Intentions

Lust is a pounce of the heart, and it pulsates through your veins quickly and powerfully. To act on the heart's impulse would be to pounce on instinct alone. Some find this easy; others find it difficult to act quickly every time you find yourself attracted to another. Lust is the prerequisite to any romantic relationship. First there must be an attraction, a desire to be more than just acquaintances or friends with the other.

Once you are romantically interested in someone, you need to ask yourself "What do I want from this?" Sometimes, the answer is simply sex. Other times, the answer is much more complicated, and that's when you need to think before you pounce. If sex is all that you desire, and you really don't see anything more between the two of you, then make sure your intentions are known. Ask the other what they are doing, create small talk that gets to a discussion of sex, and then plainly and simply ask if there is any interest.

If there is interest, *before* taking any action you will want to restate that your objective is sexual in nature and that you are not looking for more. Nothing feels worse than misleading or being misled into something where you give yourself to someone and they throw you aside when they are done with you.

Many are too shy to try and pounce on lust. If you truly want to try, you just have to go for it. Just like riding a bike, you will need to fall a few times before you get it right and ride. Even the best bike riders will fall occasionally, long after they master riding. Just get back on and go. The pounce for a lust-based relationship is not as meaningful or significant as when seeking a relationship; therefore, the thought involved does not need to be as detailed.

Befriending

The desire to seek out relationships appears to be in almost every human. Some are content with being a lone ranger in the world, but for most, sooner or later, the desire to be with someone, the desire to be loved or at least a part of something bigger, something more than just oneself, takes shape. For some, this quest for a relationship comes early in life. For others, it happens when the "biological clock" starts ticking, often in the late thirties. The common belief is that men typically look for relationships later in life and women look for marriage sometime after age seven. However, this is not always true. Mostly, the quest for a relationship has to do more with the individual's upbringing. Small town upbringing vs. city, broken home vs. tight-knit family, large vs. small family, and many other factors come into play when it comes to a person's disposition to seeking a relationship and keeping a healthy one going.

Whatever your background was, at some point you will feel the need to find that someone special to share your life with. As we grow up, you obtain "best friends." As we mature, we find "significant others." Either way, most people tend to have a few close partners in life. How we find these partners is usually by happenstance. We generally do not go out and seek a person to become friends with. Usually there is a natural transition in life whereby you gravitate toward others who are in a similar situation as you are at the same time. This person or these people may not be the best people to befriend for your long-term goals, but that is usually not the thought when friendships and relationships begin. With the pounce theory, these reactionary friendships should actually be more carefully considered. The quest for a relationship should be taken seriously and acted on to benefit your future. You should not befriend just anyone who comes along at the right time.

Once we are out of high school, it behooves us to seek out those we would like to be around versus those who are just around. When you see someone who is active and participates in events that you would like to get into or is going down a path that you would like to travel down as well, this is the time to pounce.

In my dealings with people throughout my life, I have found it quite easy to make light of the fact that the person I admire will soon be my best friend. I've walked up to people I've admired and stated, "I want you to be my best friend." It's a surprising statement to the person, but they typically are intrigued and flattered.

My reasoning generally follows up this statement. I outline why they have impressed me or why I think it would be mutually beneficial for both of us to befriend each other. I may ask to be invited to an event the other is going to. I may ask if I can be included on e-mails or in the coordination efforts of a particular event that I believe would be good to get involved with. The point is, if there are genuine feelings for more than just the person's exterior, it's easy to summarize what impresses you about them. If you see a person whom you would like to emulate or assimilate with, it becomes easier to point these facts out to that person. Nothing makes people feel better about themselves than to hear the favorable impression that others have about them. Compliments, when genuine and quantifiable, are always easily accepted and appreciated.

Now this is not to say that admiring a person for their looks is a bad thing, but you need to admire a person for what they do, what they stand for, or what they are trying to accomplish. If you do not, or there is no more than just looks to admire, you will not have a relationship or at least not one that will lead you down a path that you want. These types of relationships will go down a path of reacting to what the others do and want. This is where most people falter. Remember, stick with what you admire, and tell those that you admire what it is and why you admire them. Then be blunt; ask if you can be more involved with them in particular endeavors. More likely than not, this will lead to a relationship of some kind—romantic, possibly; fulfilling, definitely.

Have Others Beaten You to the Punch?

You may look around and you feel like you're the only one without that someone special. It feels like your friends have found someone they enjoy to hang around with, and you are left behind. This is usually a temporary feeling. Often your friends are looking right back at you thinking you have such freedom not being tied down. However, if you do feel like you are alone, this is usually an indication that you are ready to start looking for a more serious relationship. So when should you pounce?

People tend to mature at different times in life. Men often mature much later than women. Because of this phenomenon, it is widely believed that men prefer to date and marry younger women and that women generally prefer older men. However, younger or older, most agree that within five years is optimal for an age difference. Regardless of these statistics, remember that you may mature and be ready for a relationship at a different time than some of your friends or others around you.

Once you enter the workforce and work the majority of the weekday hours, you may find that most of your colleagues are married or in serious relationships. Often these coworkers got into their relationships shortly after starting in the working world, and the relationship began before the person really was prepared for a serious relationship. Quite often expectations were not set properly, which causes a demise in the relationship. What this tells you about that person is they were interested in getting into a serious relationship, they just most likely got into the wrong one or they have grown out of the current relationship. The great thing about people who have been in previous long-term relationships or marriages is that they know what they want out of a relationship—and now they know what they don't want in them. This knowledge is crucial when you are starting a new relationship.

You may discover that a compatible coworker, social interest club member, office sporting team member, or other person whom you are dealing with is in a troubled relationship with his or her partner. Someone else has beaten you to the punch and is dating or married to a person whom you see as a good match for you. Now be very careful with these next few paragraphs. I am not advocating breaking up a marriage or relationship so you can date someone. You do not want to be a home wrecker in any way. You want to be quite the opposite.

If you find that your friend is confiding in you that his or her relationship is not going the way they desire, you need to listen and then actively defend the other side. Agreeing that the other is a jerk will only make your friend want to defend their partner, and in the end, they may resent you for agreeing with them in the first place. If you take the stance that they are correct in feeling the way they do, but also point out that their partner is terrific, your friend will either insist that their partner is not great and in fact is one who needs to move on, or they will see that you are correct and made good observations, and thus you will save their relationship.

If you save their relationship, your friendship strengthens with both your friend and their partner. If your friend decides to break up or divorce, you will be the one who helped them see the light, the path to a better relationship. You will be the one who took the high road and did not just sit idle or just agree with them. You challenged them to realize what they truly desired. If they do decide to break up or divorce, you will be the one they run to, and your pounce was done without you becoming a home wrecker.

Remember, sometimes the best person to build a relationship with is someone who has had a serious relationship, or even a few, and now knows what they want in a relationship. If you two hit it off, the beautiful part is that one of you has already gotten a good understanding of what is truly important to them and knows how to make things work, or at least knows what not do so that disaster can be avoided. Have others beaten you to the punch? Hopefully—and hopefully they will have helped you out.

Consider this tactic in other situations as well. When someone is frustrated with a person or a situation, agreeing and feeding the frustration can lead down a negative path for the person confiding in you, and in turn, will lead down a negative path for your relationship. Acknowledging the issues, confirming their concerns are relevant, yet discussing other viewpoints will usually lead to a much better outcome for all parties. Out of conflicts come opportunities. There is no better time to set up the pounce than when conflict arises.

Identifying Yourself

Finding the right person to spend the rest of your life with can be and should be the most challenging yet rewarding experience you will ever undertake in your life. The problem with most people's search for love is not that they are looking in the wrong place or for the wrong people, it's that they are not proactively looking and instead take what gets handed to them. You need to "sample large." Now when we say sample large, that does not mean date everyone you see and get to know them all. Nor does it mean you must date large people. Sampling large means taking a look at what is out there. You work with many people. You see many people at school, restaurants, coffee shops, hang out spots, etc. You have met thousands of people in your life. From those thousands of people whom you have met, you have only a handful of truly great friends. Most people only have three or four really close friends. Think about these close friends. They share attributes with you that you find consoling, cordial, friendly, and, in general, desirable.

Take a close look at these individuals. Some say opposites attract; some disagree and say like people attract one another. You can see in your friends what types of people you prefer. Take a good, hard look at those you are closest to and try and itemize the attributes you share and enjoy. Particular attributes to delve into are interests and communication styles. When listing the positive attributes of all your friends, you may see a trend.

Conversation is the key to any relationship. The types of typical conversations you have with close people and also the style in which the conversations play out are important. People who talk a lot tend to befriend those who are quieter in nature. If you have two talkers, you create problems. Typically, one will dominate a conversation and one likes to listen. Communication is probably the most important attribute you need to assess in yourself and those around you. You may be a great conversationalist, and you may find other conversationalists interesting and fun to be around, but most likely, if you are a conversationalist, your close friends are not.

Pay close attention not only to the way you communicate but also to the topics you are interested in discussing. Realize that many desires in life will change as you get older; however, the fundamentals, such as interests and communication style change subtly. For example, you may be a fervent scuba diver and may be attracted to others who share the same passion for the ocean. As you get older, children, career, and others become more important factors in your life. Scuba diving may not be the passion you seek out on a weekly basis, but the love for being active and adventurous may still be an important factor in your life. Don't concentrate on the actual activities, but on the types of activities you enjoy. If you are an outdoorsy person, don't look for a mate inside a video arcade or one who sets up "dinner and movie" dates. This type of person will not provide the excitement you will need later in life. If you do enjoy movies and indoor activities, you may get excited about a date who takes you outside; but in the long run, this person might begin to feel caged up, and you may not be long-term compatible.

Assessing and knowing oneself is the key to finding that potential soul mate. If you do not know who you are and what personalities attract you, you will not be able to pounce on the opportunity to be with your potential sole mate. You will continue to hope for a reactive chance encounter and will be challenged to find true, long-term happiness. Again, what personalities attract you is much different from what personalities are attracted to you. Make sure you choose your destiny in life.

Once you make your assessment about you, consult with your best friends. When you receive good input from your family, friends, and most

73

importantly, yourself, you can then set yourself up for your own pounce. If you find you are attracted to outdoors personalities, start signing up for bicycle clubs, tennis clubs, hiking clubs, or whatever activities you enjoy. Concentrate on getting closer to those whom you enjoy activities with. If you like to travel, get into travel groups. If you enjoy dinners and movies, sign-up for dating services like Dinner for Six or other dining set up meeting groups. The point is, get active in looking for that someone special. If you think life will bring you that someone special without you exerting effort, you will end up settling for whatever comes across the plate by a certain time in life. Pounce on creating the opportunities; do not wait. You will know when the time is right to find that special person. You should participate in activities that will help you get the desired one.

Children

Children can provide the most challenging, yet most rewarding experiences in life. Many parents have difficult times coping with the day-to-day activities, the trial and tribulations of children, and their personalities. Our children are our own flesh and blood. For that reason, it is expected that they think, talk, and act like us all the time. Unfortunately, that can't be further from the truth. Children are brought up in a dramatically different society today than their parents were. Today's children must be computer literate. Video games are in every household, or so they will tell you. Television and movies have become more sophisticated and often violent or sexual in content. Most information comes from the Internet. School testing and scoring has become a greater pressure, and the need to overachieve is stronger than ever before. Competition is stronger in all aspects of life for children. No longer can a student get by with merely good athletic talent or just by being nice to the teacher.

Children have much more stress today than ever before. You, as a parent, have more stress than your parents. From the looks of things around us, the world is becoming ever more populated, crowded, and competitive. The children of tomorrow will have more leeway and liberties than today's children. At the same time, they will have more stress to compete than ever before. Your job as a parent is to tow the fine line of pushing your child to do better and being there to support when times are tough.

Children will always push your buttons, will always push the envelope of what they can get away with, will always push for more. Parents have to constantly pull them into the real world and often have to say no to their demands. How you say no and how you push them to strive for more is crucial. If you don't push them to strive for more at the right time, your children may not grow up with a passion and desire to succeed or to be significant. If you push too hard, you may cause burnout or resentment in your child and may bring them down.

There is no one pounce with children, yet a series of pounces throughout their development. As a parent, you need to be cognizant of what your child is capable of. Don't place thoughts in their head about what they are good at and what they are not. Guide them, lead them, and show them options. Have them decide what intrigues them. Let them bring their talents forward. At the same time, you must show them the world and all it has to offer. You need to show them music, science, sports, debates, and other activities and interests. They need to express a desire—a true desire—to become a musician, scientist, an athlete, whatever they are excited about, and then you can pounce. Now the pounce is not merely just getting them into a sport or buying them an instrument to play with. The pounce here is to ask and probe as to how much they want to explore the path. If they are genuinely interested and want to excel, then help them set goals and rewards:

- "If you play the piano and get good enough to perform in a small concert in front of others, we will get you …"
- "If you play soccer for one year, next year you can choose all your equipment and we'll talk to the coach about what position you would like to be placed into and worked on with."

By setting up goals and rewards, you will entice your child to perform to the best of their abilities or quickly realize that the goal is not worthwhile and the activity is not one in which they have true interest in. By pouncing on their desires, you can create motivated, driven children—but on their terms, not yours. In the end, you will have a happier and more gracious child than if you sign them up for events that they are not passionate about.

Choosing Your Battles

You've most likely heard the expression "choose your battles." Keeping quiet when the issues are not large and then pouncing on the issues closest to you is indeed the best way to pounce on the battle you choose to fight. When someone argues every issue that arises, communication breaks down and others stop listening. However, if 90 percent of the time, you are agreeable and concur with the general decision made, the one out of ten times you put your foot down, people will listen. The pushback demonstrated is unusual and thus throws everyone off. Keeping others on the edge and catching them off guard can give you a tremendous advantage.

There are other ways to not only choose your battles, but also ensure the message you are trying to convey gets across. One method that works well with children is the method of delayed ramifications. When a child starts acting up, fussing, moaning, whining, and generally acting like they are owed the world, parents often will chastise the child immediately with an inconsequential scolding. By inconsequential, we mean a scolding that the child really does not care too much about. Some parents will give the child a timeout, some will give a small spanking, others will send the child to their rooms. We've all heard of the various ways in which parents may punish their children, but does the child really and truly care about the punishment? Does the punishment correlate to the behavior? Does the child learn true consequences? You may have pounced on the bad behavior, but will the pounce be effective? Probably not. It will seem reactive and inappropriate to the bad behavior exhibited.

Here is one alternative that I have seen work well for many. Say your child starts throwing a tantrum and uses words to anger you, such as "I hate you," "I don't care," curse words, or other arguments. By sending them to their room, you may actually be rewarding them. A little quiet time away from their parents may not be much of a punishment. It may not be a big deal to sit in a corner for a few minutes for a timeout when they are bored anyway. However, taking or restricting something they really want, now there's something that they'll remember. But how do you take away something when there is nothing to take away?

Immediate punishment is the worst punishment anyone can give. It leads to rash decisions and unrelated punishments. Waiting until the right moment keeps everyone at attention and lets everyone understand what consequences come from what actions. Say a child throws a tantrum about what you are buying at a grocery store. An immediate timeout is nothing for a child bored to tears in a grocery store. However, if you say, "Stop it or you will face consequences," you may get the child's attention—especially if the child knows you will act later. If the child continues to misbehave, remember.

So a day or two later, your child wants ice cream; now's the time to pounce. By not giving in and then clarifying why your child will not be getting ice cream, this leads to "cause-and-reaction" understanding. Explain your actions to your child by stating something like this:

"Remember two days ago, when you threw a fit in the grocery store and I told you to stop or else I would not give in to your demands another day? Well today is that day, and you will not be getting any ice cream. Throw another tantrum now and in days from now, the consequences will be even greater."

Once a child sees this type of punishment a few times, they realize that actions have consequences that may not appear immediately. Banning TV when they misbehave may just lead to more boredom, which most likely they were bored to begin with, had no strong desire to watch a particular show, and thus started to misbehave. Ban TV when they want to watch because of an action that occurred days before—now that's a consequence that hurts. Punish with actions that truly make a child see that there will be consequences that they will not like, and the child can understand what they may have put you through wasn't worth it.

If you do not take action in the days after an argument, the child will always run over you. Wait too long to punish, and the child may be confused as to the reason for the punishment, and the effect is lost. The key is to not immediately pounce, but not wait too long either. One to three days maximum is the best time to pounce. When a child needs discipline, let them know, with no uncertainty, they will receive a punishment for their bad behavior. Make sure that when they want something in the next one to three days—hopefully something they really desire and something temporary—that's when you must stand your ground and say no and remind them of why you are taking your action.

By temporary, I mean short term. Don't say no to signing up for soccer for the school year just because you were upset for a moment. Take action accordingly and appropriately. If the child threw a small tantrum, take away a small item of desire. If the child contributes to a catastrophic event, then punish accordingly. If the child cries too much when it's bedtime, two days later turn off the TV early and let them know it's family time with no TV due to their behavior the other day. If a child comes home with drugs and alcohol, then banning them from seeing certain "friends," being out after 8:00 p.m. for weeks, taking them off their high school extracurricular team, or other drastic measures may be warranted.

Make sure you set the stage with others around you. Bad behavior will be remembered, will cause action to be taken, and will not be tolerated. Make sure you pounce in a timely manner and appropriately. You will find your strong words will carry weight, and quickly your children will listen or live on pins and needles waiting for the hammer to fall and a real consequence to happen.

Sports and Recreation

Get Your Game Face On

Sports have often been used in metaphors and analogies about life and working relationships. Sports are where true competition and strategy can be displayed. Teamwork is usually a key element in sports, as are persistence, strength, willpower, drive, determination, and many other attributes. All of these attributes can be in your portfolio of strengths; however, without an understanding of when to pounce, you may end up on the losing end of the game more often than not.

When sizing up your competition, you need to get into your opponent's mind-set. Will they rely on their strength to try and overpower you, or will they use finesse to outshine and outperform your team? Of course, many of these questions depend on the sport you are engaged in, but regardless of what sport, your opponent has a strategy for winning and so do you. Who will be the ultimate victor is dependent on who pushes forward at the right time—not too soon in the match, but not too late, after the game has been decided, either.

Understanding the pounce in sports quite often can translate to understanding your competition at work, school, or other aspects in life. Getting your game face on merely means focusing on the strategy and methodologies you will need to use to ultimately win the match.

Prior to the start of a game, one team or some individuals may engage in "trash talking." This is where the trash-talking team or individual is looking to gain a psychological advantage by boosting their psyche and demeaning the competition. The thought process is that the competition will either lose confidence or will become so enraged that they will become emotional and lose focus, thus becoming more likely to lose the match.

Trash Talking is for those who have nothing else to gain but humiliation. Though some will disagree, trash talking generally invokes emotions in the players who are not as focused and not as good as most. Trash talking is very effective against those who are not dominant in the sport. However, trash talking to someone who is dominant may just stir a stronger desire to perform better and humiliate the talker. To effectively pounce, you need to assess your opponent. Is this individual strong, weak, good in adverse situations, easily frustrated, etc.? Professional athletes will review videotapes of opposing teams to look for their weaknesses and to see how to avoid their strengths. These are the questions that need to be answered before you pounce, especially before you engage in trash talk.

At the core of the pounce theory is timing. In order to time your pounce correctly, you need to assess and measure up your opponent. In boxing, this technique is quite common. Verbal sparring takes place months in advance, however, once the bell sounds and the first round begins, the boxers do not engage in any dialogue or trash talking. Instead, they mostly dance around and throw a few jabs. The first round is usually boring to watch, yet crucial for each boxer to "size the other up."

When you begin your game, you need to mirror your opponent. If you are truly better than them, it will not matter that you didn't pounce right away. However, if your opponent is good at the sport and can hold their own, you may have a formidable challenge ahead, and the pounce will be critical. Even if you find your opponent to be superior in ability than you, a correct pounce can prove victorious in the end. Stamina and willpower can favor you even if the opponent is much better.

Conditioning is key, and the better shape you are in for the sport, the more likely success will come to you. However, conditioning is often a matter of time and practice put into the sport. With our hectic lifestyles, unless you are in school or a professional athlete, it may be difficult to put the time into a sport to become as accomplished as you would like. This does not mean you can't win every time you engage, it just means you need to be in tune with your weaknesses and know when to pounce.

I will refer to a physical ordeal that I underwent a number of years ago. My friends and I decided we would do the "Death Ride." The bike ride consisted of going from the lowest point in the continental United States to the highest point in the continental United States. That meant a bike ride of 140 miles from Badwater, Death Valley, to the base of Mount Whitney, followed by a 14-mile hike to the top of Mount Whitney. In total, the ride involved 18,000 feet of vertical bike climbing and 5,000 feet of vertical hiking. Fortunately, my friends felt it would take three to four days to accomplish this feat. My friends had trained for this extraordinary bike ride for months. I had minimal time and thus spent minimal amount of training hours to prepare for the event. Of the four of us, I was clearly the weakest bike rider and in the worst physical condition. However, I treated the event as a game, and I knew a strategic pounce would be crucial if I wanted to finish first—or even finish, for that matter.

The first day of our ride was uneventful; however, I was consistently the last rider and well back of the pack the whole day. The second day, I noticed the others getting fatigued. I stayed behind most of the day and only began to ride with the pack at the end of the day. Before the sun set and the day was complete, I pounced. I mustered up the last bits of my biking strength and forged ahead. I made it to the base of Mount Whitney three hours before the second person rode to the point and the other two hitchhiked the last part due to fatigue, nightfall, and mechanical problems.

The next day, I was elated with the energetic burst I had displayed the day before. I pounced at the right time, and the others felt defeated. The will to finish strong was diminished for them and strengthened for me. The third day, I insisted on hiking all the way to the top. The others felt we should camp midway; we agreed I would meet them there. I hiked to the top of Mount Whitney and returned to the campsite by nightfall. The others were in their tents preparing for the next day. I had completed the task one day ahead of schedule, and played the game to my success. It turned out, the next day I waited at the bottom of the mountain in a warm restaurant. The mountain was shut down to hikers because of dangerously high winds. The three could not complete the hike or the end goal. I was the only one to complete the mission, and to this day, among my friends, am still the only one. It is a sore topic of discussion; however, it is an example of how a good pounce can help you accomplish your goals. I relay this story not to brag about my physical prowess, but more to demonstrate a time when the pounce was indeed critical for me to not only "win" in the game I contrived, but to even complete a goal that I, and others, had set out for ourselves.

When engaging in a particular sport, you need to look at all the parameters of the sport. Is the sport an endurance trail or a speed test? Is there scoring involved, or is it a judged sport? What will the outcome of the game be in terms of will the team be ranked or listed in standings, or will there just be a point total at the end of the season for all wins? The importance of these questions is in the strategy that needs to be taken to effectively invoke your pounce.

Endurance sports will need a bit of the tortoise and the hair approach in that the pounce will need to be well timed and strategy will be essential. Too soon and you will burn out, and the win will go to your opponent. Pounce too late of and you will never catch up in time. Conversely, a speed-oriented sport may require a quick pounce; perhaps setting doubt in your opponents mind before the gun goes off might bode well for you. A display of confidence or even a small amount of trash talk may work.

In sports that are scored, a quick start and overpowering display of dominance can often squish your competitions desire to or will to compete. However, consistency or minimally a strong finish will need to be thought about. Arrogance after a quick start may lead to complacency, and a sneak attack by the opponent at the last minute might result in your loss. When scoring is involved, score quick and often, and then make sure the lead is kept at a certain threshold. If the lead dwindles beyond a comfortable margin, bring back the starters, call timeout and get the needed rest, or do whatever your strategy calls for to win or score.

Judged sports are subjective and rely on a panel of judges to provide scoring or determine the winner by vote. These judges are experts in the sport and know who the better performers in the sport are. This will usually play a role to some extent in their scoring or voting. For judged sports, the pounce is well before the performance. Understanding what the judges are looking for and crafting your performance to bring out your strengths as well as play to the judges likes will be critical and the key to scoring well. Get to know your judges, whether by reputation or by actually talking to them. It is much more difficult to judge harshly if you know the person and have engaged in conversation with them and know you will again.

Often in life, we need to challenge ourselves and perhaps artificially create a game out of the task at hand. Whether it is for a fun event, a worthy cause, or even work that needs to be done, a difficult task can be more easily handled if it is viewed as a game. It is at these times that one needs to think about not only the end goal at hand, but also when the proper time to pounce is. If you create a game and improperly pounce, your morale and ego may be deflated, and you may give up rather than succeed. Your game face can be put on for any event; however, don't show your cards until the others do. In other words, do not show your game face, or even an interest in the game, until pounce time, and then go all out.

Pounce Time

You may be asking, "Just when is that pounce time, and how will I know when it has arrived?" This is a question you will be able to answer when the time appears. It is plain to see if you are paying attention. In the first chapter, we discussed the "state of mind" you should always be in. When competing in a game of any kind, you need to be conscientious of your opponents at all times. Never keep your eyes off them; watch their eyes if possible. In my quest to ride to Mount Whitney and complete the Death Ride, I never allowed my opponents to leave my sight, or at least not for very long. Striking distance had to be known at all times. Likewise, pounce time will be obvious to you if you continually assess your opponent and look into their eyes regularly.

Fatigue shows in many ways. Mostly, we associate sweat with fatigue. However, droopy eyelids, dangling lower arms, dragging feet, slower lateral movements, slower turns of the head—these are all indications of fatigue. Heavy breathing and hands clasping to the shorts are well known signs of a fatiguing basketball player. Football quarterbacks show fatigue by more persistent underthrows rather than overthrowing to the wide receivers. Soccer players often show none of these signs, rather, they just stop running for open spots when fatigued. In all sports, there are telltale signs of fatigue that could be used to the detriment of the opponent, however, they are rarely identified by others playing in the game. You may hear announcers stating that a player is fatigued. The coaches may see it as well and substitute someone else in place of the fatigued player. Players on the field rarely see others fatiguing, since they themselves are often undergoing the same stresses.

Great players understand not only the game, but the pounce. Great players see the opponent and know what side is their weak side versus their strong side. Great players know when their opponent is fatigued and the weaknesses that can be exploited once fatigue is shown.

This once again shows the importance of the proper pounce. If you play the game right, you will not allow yourself to fatigue as others do. Play good defense and keep the game close. Do not go for the quick win, but you may want to go for the quick score. Eventually, you will see fatigue setting in to your opponent. This is the time to pounce. Few teams have ever won the Super Bowl on offense alone.

The championship games usually have the best offense versus the best defense in the league that year. The best defense will almost always win. I personally cannot remember ever seeing a game where the better defense did not win the championship. The best defense may lose some games, but they usually win the ultimate game. A good offence may be exciting and keep your team scoring, but eventually the opponent will stop you or slow you down. Fatigue may set in. A good defense will stop the other team from coming back. A great defense provides opportunities for the offense. Simply, the better defense allows the team or individual to stay in the game for the proper time to pounce. Defense allows you to hold the opponent in check so that the offense can quickly kick into action and pounces enough to win the game. Good defense is designed to keep you in the game; however, the win is in the timing and the power of the pounce.

Shopping

Every day, we face dozens of choices, often choices that feel mundane, yet can make or break our day, week, or immediate future. These choices, if made without much thought, can lead to challenges, extra costs, or regrets. Taking a moment to think about your choices and acting in a manner that will lead you down the path of least resistance can be considered a good pounce. Planning and preparation are the key elements of a successful pounce. Planning and preparation can start from the most simple steps.

There are things we do every day or every week that, if done with purpose, can yield far better results than if we continued conducted ourselves in the way we did before the pounce. Let's take shopping as an example of an activity that we all do on a consistent basis. Simply shopping for merchandise can seem routine. You have a need, you go to the store, you purchase what you need—done. However, retail purchases, large item purchases like cars and houses, travel plans, and other purchases should take thought and planning. After all, this is your money and your time you are investing in the purchase. Make sure you look for a pounce opportunity and capitalize as much as you can from your shopping. Let's take a look at some areas that can become more effective if a pounce is considered.

Retail Shopping

Supply and demand is what allows capitalism and free enterprise to exist. It is truly the only way freedom can exist. However, supply and demand is considered mostly a macroeconomic philosophy. This means that supply and demand is a relative term used to describe economics as a whole. However, supply and demand exists on a micro level as well. The most microeconomic view one can have is in one's own personal spending. Here, supply and demand is the most beneficial to you as the consumer. When you are engaged in a negotiation or sale of a product, you are the only demander of that product with the salesperson. Even red-hot goods that everyone is buying are only being demanded by one person when you are negotiating with a salesperson. This is a revelation that cannot be overlooked.

Time is critical to every salesperson. Every minute that a salesperson has, is a minute that he or she can be making a sale, and in turn, be making money. All salespeople appreciate easy windfall sales; however, if you make them work for the sale, suddenly, the odds are in your favor. Let's look at it from the salesperson vantage point. Say you are engaged in a sales process for an item that you are interested in buying. If you state that you would like the item for various reasons, the salesperson does not need to say anything. Showing the value of the product is all being done by you, the buyer. You are selling the item to yourself, and thus you may work yourself into a need frenzy. Good salespeople know and understand this and will merely help you sell yourself on the product.

If, however, you ask the salesperson to show you the value of the product, now you are making them earn their sales. I am neither against salespeople, nor do I wish to create difficulties for any of them. However, I would like to see a working knowledge of the product they are selling and indeed a deserved sales commission if they can successfully show me value in the product. Just to clarify, value is and can only be perceived by the buyer. The salesperson can only direct the buyer to see the value. The salesperson cannot prove value to any buyer, only the buyer can know of any item's true value to themselves.

Once value is agreed upon, the sale is complete and only the monetary transaction remains. However, the more time you spend with the salesperson, the more the salesperson will need to make the sale. For example, if a salesperson grabs your attention and asks you about your interest in a certain item, no time has really lapsed. If you state you are interested and would like to buy the product, the salesperson has invested little time in the sale and will quote you the retail or highest price possible for maximum commissioned revenue. If, however, you ask the salesperson about the product, engage in a dialogue about the various benefits of the product, and even discuss the possible outcome and alternative uses of the product, suddenly, the salesperson has invested time in the sale. To justify the time spent with you, the salesperson must make a sale. The salesperson could have spent his or her time with someone else and made a sale. The salesperson will not want to lose the deal at this point and will begin to ask what price is acceptable to you. They may ask directly, they may probe in a roundabout manner, they may even quote you a price. However low it may be, the price will not be completely set.

Once the negotiation begins, it is imperative to once again consume as much time as needed and completely understand the benefits and the value of the product. This will drive a salesperson crazy as the sales process is now taking more time than initially anticipated. If the salesperson addresses someone else or walks away, the salesperson then has invested more time than desired and has walked away with nothing. Rather than leave empty-handed, most salespeople will resort to bargaining or haggling for your business. It is at this moment that you have the upper hand.

The salesperson may ask you what it will take for you to buy the item today. Employee discounts run from 10 percent to 40 percent for any item. There are also coupons for many items, including garments and luxury items. Often we see buy one get one free. We see 50 percent off the second item when you spend more than $100. These are only examples, however, "deals" exist on almost all goods sold. Most people do not take advantage of these offers simply because they are not informed or they feel that they do not qualify for them. Over the entire day or week, the store will take in many more profits from people who do not take advantage of these deals. This is where the savvy customer can negotiate.

Throughout the week, other shoppers have not taken the discounts they could have received. Knowing that the salesperson can mark down any item in any store is valuable. Telling the salesperson that you can buy the item for a 25 percent discount, equaling the employee discount, or equaling a coupon that is out in the general public will be to your benefit. Almost all stores have a preferred pricing list that is lower to the few people who "qualify" for the pricing. There is no reason you cannot ask to be one of those people. By stating your case and further engaging the salesperson in more conversation, now you have occupied the salesperson to an extent that they will want to cut their losses. Giving you a discount of any magnitude will get you out of the store a happy customer, the item will be sold, and the store will profit. Keeping you in the store to haggle the price more only hurts the salesperson's chances of making another sale. At this point, the salesperson will often buckle and give you a substantial discount.

Some stores have salespeople on a straight salary and pay no commissions. Don't be fooled into thinking the salespeople have no incentive to sell. If their section of products and goods do not move or turn at a certain rate, it reflects poorly on the salespeople in that section. I have had great success at stores like Best Buy, Fry's, and other electronics stores, as well as Gap, Kohl's, Macy's, Nordstrom, and many more stores that tout their salespeople are not commissioned. Salespeople are hired to do one thing: sell, not waste time chatting with people and letting them walk out of the store and buy elsewhere. Let the salesperson earn their pay and do their job. There are discounts to be had on every product, why shouldn't you be able to take advantage of that?

Never feel that you need a product so badly that you sell it to yourself. Even the hottest products will have one salesperson devoted to you at any given time. Use their time and watch the price fall. No salesperson can justify spending one hour with a customer only to have them walk away without a sale. Sales managers will eat the salesperson alive if they hear of such acts. Utilize a salespersons time effectively, and more often than not, you will be able to negotiate down the price of the item or get more for your money. Remember, for that salesperson, you are the only demander standing in front of them. Having a supply and only one demander, you can command the price if you spend the time.

Car Buying and Large Ticket Purchases

Most adults will purchase a car more than a few times in his or her life. A car is usually the second largest purchase made after a house. Most people will spend more than forty hours researching, test driving, analyzing, and price shopping before purchasing a car. With large purchases like real estate and cars, negotiation is almost always a necessary evil. Don't cringe or shy away from the negotiation table. Embrace the fact that you have an opportunity to negotiate and get the most out of your large purchase. Remember, getting the most may not be lowest price, but perhaps it means having more accessories "thrown in." Don't let the salesperson be the one with the pounce. This will lead to buyer's remorse, and with cars and homes, that feeling can last for many years.

As in most retail sales operations, the end of the month and end of the quarter are extremely important when it comes to accounting and analyzing growth and profitability. The more sales and revenue, the better the managers look, as well as the business itself. Profitability is key, but at the end of the quarter, revenue is king. Managers want to show that they have increased, or at least did not decrease, in overall revenue sales from the previous quarter or last year's same quarter. Growth allows for more hiring or build-outs of facilities or other positive allowances. Often growth is rewarded with commissions or bonuses. Should the quarter end lower than the last or flat, negative changes could be made to the management structure or payouts could be negatively affected. Understanding this allows you to time your pounce. Test drive cars, attend open houses, tour boat shows—whatever large ticket item you are researching, do what research you need to do during the first two months of any quarter. Buy toward the end of the quarter.

Whether you shop for clothes or cars, the end of the quarter is deal time. The difference between clothes and cars, though, is that clothing purchases matter on a much smaller scale. One person will not make much difference in the clothing world, but you are spending tens of thousands of dollars for your car. With real estate, hundreds of thousands or more will be spent. Dealers, brokers, and retailers have made their profits through the first two months of the quarter. Some may even hold out for midmonth in the third month before desperation sets in and the deals need to be made at almost any cost.

You see, if a dealership sells one car at a very profitable price per quarter, that may look good for margins, but the revenue just isn't there. Car dealers get credits or "holdbacks" from the manufacturers based on how much they sell. Large dealers get more holdbacks and thus get more in profit. Large dealers also get revenue streams for years as the cars need to be serviced, and many people go back to the dealer to get their cars repaired. There are many more items that go into the revenue category in terms of perks the dealer gets when they sell more. So if you sell one car a quarter with a lot of profit, the dealership will not be around for very long. If the dealer sells one car for a lot of profit and then sells one thousand cars for zero profit, in the end, the dealer will make more money because of the credits they will receive from the manufacturer that sends them rebates for the quantity of cars they sold. Also, of the other one thousand cars sold, many will return for repairs and maintenance items for years to come. So even though the profit seems to be the same, the long-term money flow is greater when the dealer sells more, even at a low profit margin for a few deals.

Understanding this can go a long way. With a little research and knowledge, you can save thousands of dollars in the negotiation process when buying a car. If you conduct your test drives early in the quarter and hone down on the exact make and model, now all that's left is the negotiation. When you walk into a dealership, start by emphasizing that you do not have much time and you are a no-nonsense customer looking for a deal today. You are now talking the salesperson's talk, and you appear to be a dream customer. But with one or two days left in the quarter, you are in the driver's seat.

Make sure you have done your research, have a price in your head of what you feel is reasonable to expect, and then lower that price 5–10 percent and start there. Now you are ready to start your pounce. Ask for your car with the features you desire. Let the salesperson know that you've done your homework and that you have another dealership looking for your car at the price you want. Let the salesperson know that a manager is welcomed to join in on the discussion, because you only have one hour to get the price and sign, or you will need to come back later. This sets up a hurried atmosphere, and in an environment where stress is high to get the deal, managers and salespeople often drop their price much quicker than when they have a little more time to think. Price slashing is easy; value selling is more difficult. If you control the rushed atmosphere, you have the upper hand in the negotiations.

Once you reach a price—even if it is the price you wanted—leave. Leave with a smile on your face, and be very polite. State that you have to leave for a quick engagement but that you'll be back shortly to sign the deal and move forward. The staff will not want you to leave. They may drop their price even further just to entice you not to leave. They will want you to sign a holding agreement. Just keep smiling and state, "I'll be back soon, and we'll finish then. I must leave. Thank you."

Always leave. If you feel you got the best price ever, go back in twenty minutes and let them know that the engagement was cancelled. Otherwise, you can return hours later, or go to another dealer to ensure you are getting the best deal. Once you return, the deal has been done. No matter how often they say we can only give this deal to you now, the deal will be available later. You may hear, "If you leave, we may not be able to guarantee this price." They will not raise the price and risk losing the deal altogether. They will accept the last negotiated price to finalize and get you out as soon as possible. If you are afraid to leave or negotiate, you will leave money on the table. The pounce is setting up the final negotiation and then leaving. If you stick to your guns, you will save a substantial amount. If you are feeling sorry for the dealer, remember, they will get their credits later and the salesperson will get their commissions, especially with the quarter-end promotions they usually receive. Everyone will win—only you will win more.

Travel

Traveling can be a rewarding experience, especially if the travel is for pleasure. However, setting up the flights, booking the hotels, car rentals, etc., can be exhausting. Actually going through the travel experience can be even worse. Once again, proper planning and execution can make the experience much more rewarding. Pounce on the hospitality industry, and let it work for you.

In my experience, two items distinguish what airline I fly and what flight I book. If you can travel direct, the time you save and the agony you spare yourself versus the time wasted in layovers generally pays for the slight bump in fare you may have to pay. Flying direct means you need to research what airline has the main stop as a hub or main routing point. Most airlines will route passengers to their hub and then send you on to your destination, much like FedEx treats their packages. To pounce on the right flight, you need to take the right airline that travels to the destination the most.

The second item that causes the most travel headaches and stress is weather. Often, airline will travel through Denver (United Airlines hub), Minneapolis (Northwest hub), or Chicago (American & United Airlines hub) as their midpoint or hub. In winter, these airports can have catastrophic snow delays. In summer, rains and wind wreak havoc at these airports. Flying over the Rocky Mountains can be unsettling as well. Most people think there is not much one can do in regards to weather. Mother Nature does have a mind of her own. However, traveling through hubs in southern regions, such as Phoenix (US Airways hub), Houston (Continental Airlines hub), Dallas (American Airlines hub), or Atlanta (Delta hub) to name a few, can save you many delays and headaches. Lightning storms and tornadoes can cause problems in some of these areas; however, the chances are far less than if you go through Minneapolis, Chicago, or other midcontinental northern cities.

The most important item to think about before making domestic travel arrangement is the season. Just like going to lunch at eleven thirty instead of twelve o'clock allows you to beat the lunch crowd and long waits in lines or to get a table, air travel has seasons, and booking your tickets in less peak times of the year can save you money, time, hassle, and headaches. When you have a family, these less stressful times often cannot be avoided without taking your child out of school, but it is worth mentioning for pre-child or post-child years. The pounce for domestic travel really lies in timing.

There are many deals out there, but these are not considered a pounce-type scenario. You can call rental car companies and ask if they offer free car rentals to return vehicles to their original locations. You can go online and purchase tickets to destinations on auction from people who booked nonrefundable tickets and will sell them for pennies on the dollar, or purchase tickets that the airlines are dumping to fill the airplanes. Sites like SkyAuction.com, offandaway.com, or even eBay.com can simplify the auction process. Be careful to look at the number of airline stops, the rating of the hotels, and the class of cars you are requesting before purchasing from these sites. There are deals out there for the budget travelers, but to pounce on the travel ticket, one needs to look at timing, seasons, and connection points to make a relatively low-stress travel arrangement.

International travel is far different from domestic travel. Not only for the obvious reasons of dealing with different countries and cultures, but for the mere fact that airlines and travel authorities operate much differently abroad than they do in the United States. One of the most glaring differences is that the longer you wait to purchase an airline ticket, the lower the cost is on many airlines. The theory is that if the flight has not sold out by the days prior to departure, the airline needs to lower their prices or else risk empty seats, which would fetch even less revenue for the airline.

This strategy makes sense and thus behooves travelers to wait before booking their trips while keeping in mind that popular destinations and times could get sold out in advance, and the last minute traveler may not be able to purchase a ticket. This method is used all over the world. In Asia, many travelers purchase one-way tickets to Bangkok, Thailand. They then go to the travel agents in Bangkok and purchase the remaining tickets at the last minute to go wherever they need to within Asia. In Europe, many travelers wait until the last minute or they track the loading of airplanes by calling into the airlines and asking for the loading details. The airlines will tell the passenger if the loading appears to be getting full or if there is plenty of room. Depending on how booked the flight is, the passenger will continue to wait or purchase a ticket at that time.

In other parts of the world, similar situations will be present. The airline industry changes from year to year, and the methods of obtaining deals may vary at times. The key to the pounce with international travel is flexibility. There are many fabulous destinations to go for vacation. If you are set on a particular place, waiting for prices to drop may cost you the trip altogether. If you are flexible enough to enjoy Asia, Europe, or wherever without being locked into a particular city, there are ways to work the system so that you can save substantial amounts of money. This will allow you to spend more on the destination, rather than on getting to the destination. Your travels will be more rewarding yet more spontaneous. Care for an adventure, look for the last minute deals. Looking to relax, you may want to pounce early, spend the extra money, and not worry about anything.

In General

Drama Is for Television Shows

Many of us often feel as if misfortune, hectic schedules, and overwhelming problems are placed upon us. We feel that the world does not understand our situation and what we are going through. When someone comes along and asks, "How are you?" sometimes some of us feel it is our duty to fill this person in on every detail to ensure they understand all of our issues. We can drone on and on about everything in our lives that has gone or is going wrong, but we rarely stop and think about what others go through.

"Drama queens" or persons who go on about their own problems without concern for others are often entertaining, yet annoying for long durations. Dramatic people tend to make friends quickly, because initially, they seem to understand what we all face day-to-day. Often, these dramatic people are an outlet for many of our own frustrations. They can either demonstrate that our lives are not that bad, or they can empathize with us since they, too, are going through similar experiences. In the long run, we tend to find out that drama queens have similar experiences with everyone that has a bad experience. In fact, most dramatic people have so much drama in their lives, they can never have a positive reaction to anything. Even when they do feel something good has happened, in the long run, drama queens complain about the good things.

We all have our own personal agendas in life. As life happens, those agendas need to be altered. Many of us forgo extravagant travels due to money or children or many other reasons. Some get into careers that we

96

never intended on in high school. Others go down paths in life that are far different from what we initially plan on when we were five years of age. Often times in our lives, family and friends pass away. Pets come and go, friends move on, and life changes without asking us for permission. We all share pain and suffering to a certain degree.

I am certainly not advocating keeping all your frustrations and sad stories to yourself. These experiences need to be discussed so others can realize what you are going through. This also fulfills a desire to talk with others to help develop a better understanding or even closure on experiences. However, there are ways to discuss your issues and frustrations without complaining incessantly about mundane topics. The segregation of life's setbacks and day-to-day whining needs to be carefully thought of before spewing all of your feelings. Granted, after a sudden traumatic shock or loss of a close relationship, you are allowed and expected to spew your feelings. However, frustrations about work, coworkers, family members, friends, and worldly situations and circumstances need to be carefully assessed before one goes into great detail about how bad the world is or how bad life treats you. General whining can negatively affect your future ability to pounce on an opportunity if you develop a reputation of being a negative person.

Every one of us feels strongly about numerous topics. We all have opinions. There are many appropriate avenues to vent or share these opinions. However, vocalizing these opinions to the wrong groups or individuals could have a negative impact on your current situation. Whining about world politics or the boss at work merely shows that you are not satisfied and wish to gripe to the world. This complaining does not complete anything constructive and will not bode well for you in the long run. People either shut you out of conversations, turn away from you when you really need to talk, or pass along your negative information to those who should not be privy to the knowledge that you are not pleased with the current situation. When word about your displeasure with the boss gets back to your boss, life suddenly becomes much more difficult.

Drama queens often fall into this cycle but do not understand why life is so difficult. The more they complain, the more difficult life gets, the more empathy they expect, the more they complain about life … and on it goes. If you are currently in this cycle, you need to break the habit. If you see tendencies of these behaviors, watch them and try to corral these behaviors. When one complains about issues, people will listen, but only for so long and only so many times. If you complain too much, you have a "boy who cried wolf" scenario. After a while, even real issues fall on deaf ears. Your ability to pounce is reduced or nonexistent.

If you truly want people to listen to your problems and opinions, make sure they are real problems that are tangible and relatable. Problems should be a genuine concern to you, where if you continue to keep the problem capsulated to yourself, no progress can be made. In these cases, by all means, share them with those you feel closest to or those who may be able to help. If you feel compelled to share an opinion, make sure it is relatable to the person you are discussing it with. Don't insist on animal rights to a zoologist. Most likely, you will be in complete agreement and all you are creating is small talk. Conversely, try to avoid controversial topics, such as religion, politics, and sexual topics, unless you are in the appropriate arena. These controversial topics can lead to an abundance of emotions and opinions about you that you may not want everyone to have.

When you declare all your problems and opinions to the world, over time, the world begins to shut you out. You no longer have the ability to pounce or make any kind of compelling statement. You must think about what you say at all times. With articulate speech and crisp dialogue patterns, you can convey your desires and needs effectively. People tend to react in a quick and compelling manner. Positive action gets taken instead of just listening or shutting out. Not all your speaking needs to be direct and to the point. Small talk is an important social skill and should be utilized appropriately and often if needed; however, whining and overemphasizing problems should be avoided. Make sure your small talk does not turn into whining.

One way to ensure this is to continually ask how the other person feels about what you are saying. Ask what they feel or think and if they are going through similar experiences. Ask open-ended questions to those you talk to and get them engaged in the conversation. You will find that they have much more to offer you than when you just talk on your own. You will also set yourself up to be heard when you really need to be heard. That is the essence of setting up for the pounce.

Remembering Birthdays

Birthdays are amazing days. They are days to celebrate the life of someone close to you, including yourself. Birthdays commemorate the day of a person's birth and all the joys they have brought to the world. Remember a birthday, and you are acknowledging that person's existence and stating that they are important to you. Remembering someone's birthday is possibly the most important personal gesture you can make to a person, for this was the most important day in their lives: the day they were born.

In today's technological age, there really is no excuse to forget birthdays. With smartphones, handheld personal digital assistants (PDAs), computers, social-networking websites, printed organizers and calendars, there are many ways to capture someone's birthday, write it down, and transfer it year after year. With these tools, you have the capability to remind yourself when people's birthdays are and acknowledge them for their entire life. A simple card in the mail, an e-card, or even better, a personal phone call can go a long way. When you remember a person's birthday, they will cherish that feeling you gave them. The feeling of importance and being noted is an amazing feeling. Most people will only be remembered on their birthday by a handful of people. These people will be held in the highest regard for at least one month, if not for an entire year. Simply calling someone on their birthday can make a positive impact on both of your lives for many years to come.

When we talk about setting up for the pounce, we are not saying you must pounce or see everyone as a pounce opportunity. We are merely noting that when we need something—attention, an action, or to be heard—we want the greatest opportunity to receive our request. By acknowledging people's birthdays, you will be regarded as someone with empathy who cares for them. In times of need, be it a job, a companion, anything, friends will flock to your side, especially if you are one of the few that remembers their birthday year after year. A small gesture can be very powerful. You may not see the power of birthday notes or calls for years; however, it does not take much effort, and in the long run, the rewards are great.

Now the trick in remembering people's birthday is also in the way that you obtain the information. Don't just go asking all your friends when their birthday is, although you can if you have a reason to do so. Rather, listen and observe. Look when they flash their driver's license. Listen for when they say their birthday is going to be. Ask where they were born, and see if they offer more information. Befriend them on social-networking websites that have their personal information and content. Be patient in getting this information. Over years, you will accumulate hundreds of birthdays. Do not delete these from your data banks or calendars. Keep writing them into the next year's calendars. Some people will fall out of contact, but you never know when they come back into your life. I have had people tell me they are going to see someone I once knew. I let them know if their birthday is coming up. It usually gets back to the individual that I remembered their birthday. It has never hurt, but often has helped. If you want to ensure future successes, remembering birthdays and sending a brief, friendly acknowledgment is one of the easiest opportunities to set yourself up positively with people.

E-mail

E-mail is relatively new to the world, yet it has proliferated into business and personal life like no other form of communication ever before. With this new technology, information sending and gathering has proliferated to an extent of thousands of times more information available to everyone at any moment. Many of us get inundated with hundreds of e-mails a day. Junk mail has been taken to new heights. Terms like spam no longer apply only to fake ham loafs, but to mass amounts of unwanted and unwarranted mail in our e-mail servers. Getting through the clutter can take a considerable amount of time.

Getting noticed with e-mail and getting your message across takes careful consideration. Many mass mailers use catchy lines that try to entice e-mail readers to open their message. Some e-mailers want to sell you products or services; some just want to infect your system with a virus. Whatever the catchy phrase they use, most e-mails will go unread by the intended e-mail recipient. Most will be deleted without reading or will be screened by software utilities that check for e-mail spam and delete it before the reader even gets a chance to view the e-mails.

Most communicating through e-mail or texts is to your friends and business relationships. Hopefully, you are not on the list of e-mail spammers that are screened. Assuming this, you will still need to get to the intended reader. Even if the intended reader is your best friend or close coworker, e-mails can go unread for days or get deleted due to the massive amount of e-mails people get these days. Friends and coworkers may figure they will talk to you instead of replying to your e-mail. Time goes by, and the subject is forgotten. Clearly if the issue is critical, you won't let it fall to the wayside. However, you may not get the quick response you were hoping for either.

How do you ensure you get an appropriate, timely response through e-mail these days? Use e-mail and texts appropriately. Pounce when needed; don't spam. If you categorize your e-mail for your recipients, you will make it easier for them to read and, if needed, respond. Response when needed is critical in today's business climate. Inundating friends with jokes and useless information will diminish your e-mail importance and limit the effectiveness of your e-mail communications. Categorize your e-mails and texts. Start all e-mails with "FYI:," or "Joke:," or "Need to know:." When you categorize all of your communications, your responders will become used to your filing methods and will get to your informational or humorous e-mails at the appropriate times. They will also get to your "important" or "response needed" e-mails right away.

Remember, e-mails leave a permanent record in writing. Voice inflections, sarcasm, and smiles do not come across e-mails very well. Make sure that your e-mails count. The essence of the pounce is making every moment count, even if it is a personal contact via electronic communication like e-mails and text messages. The pounce is about timing; when e-mails go unanswered because you failed to prioritize your e-mail request, you may suffer. If you need answers, set yourself up to receive them as soon as possible.

Conclusion

Seize the Moment

Seize the moment by planning the moment. Don't rush out and pounce. Like a cat stalking its prey, wiggle your tail, tuck your ears back, and keep a low profile until it's time to pounce. A cat is not trained to pounce; it's instinctive and learned through mistakes. Use some of the tools mentioned throughout this book, and concentrate on your pounce. You will find that over time you will get better at gauging people, personalities, and the proper time to pounce. Eventually, it will become second nature, but only if you concentrate and learn from the lessons of others and your own mistakes. Without lessons learned, capitalizing on your pounce will feel and come off as awkward.

Capitalizing on your efforts involves two types of examination, one prior to the pounce and one afterward. Prior to the pounce, you need to make sure you are set for the pounce. Take the steps outlined in this book and assess for yourself what steps need to be taken. Do your homework and research. Write out your goals and desires, and concentrate on the journey to obtain your goals.

The other key point in capitalizing on your efforts is to inspect the last time you pounced and the end results. Did you come on too strong? Did you ask for your desires to be met too soon? Did you get everything you wanted out of the pounce? If you did, think about what key elements transpired to make the pounce so effective. If everything did not go as smoothly as anticipated, ask yourself what could be improved?

What If the Pounce Doesn't Work?

Just like when we first learned to walk, first learned to ride a bike, first learned to excel in school or work, we will make mistakes, mistimed pounces, and fail to recognize potential opportunities to maximize our circumstances. The only advantage we have now over the times we first learned to walk is that we can now assess more intelligently what happened and how we can improve. Life is a series of learning steps. A mistimed pounce is a great learning lesson—a great first step. Pick yourself up, and think about what you missed and what could have gone better.

Often times, it's a matter of forcing a situation that just may not be there. I've seen too many times someone determined to pounce on a situation regardless of whether it is the right time. With dogged determination, they feel the conversation is almost there, and so they go for the pounce, when in fact the conversation never lent itself to the true moment for the pounce. The person merely wished it so badly that they saw signs that were not there, and they heard what they wanted to hear. These are times when we need to look back and determine if we were too overzealous. Other times, people are too timid. They are shy and have difficulties asking someone a question that could be potentially embarrassing. Often, the person never sees the opportunity to pounce, even though it presents itself numerous times.

If the pounce does not work for these or other reasons, the key is to dust yourself off and really take a moment to think about what was said, what was displayed, and what the outcome was. If the outcome was short of desired, you really need to assess if the desired outcome was or is even possible. My observations are that 90 percent of the time, the desired outcome is possible, but the pounce was not executed correctly and thus did not work. Figure out where the conversation went sideways, and remember that for the next encounter.

I say 90 percent because sometimes when you want to pounce, you find information that sets you back. This means it is time to regroup and try later. Say you want to ask someone out for a date. In talking about fun activities, you find that he or she has just started a relationship with someone. Be very interested, learn more, and then regroup and try again later with better knowledge of the situation. That was the 10 percent chance circumstance, that something from left field became known and changed the timing of the pounce. However, most of the time, the pounce is lost because we felt the time was not right, or we forced the time when it wasn't right and the pounce did not work. These are the times that we need to replay the conversations in our minds, replay the circumstances surrounding the pounce, and rethink a new strategy, new time, or new way of trying the pounce again.

It can be easy to recover if a pounce does not go well. Don't feel that you have one pounce and a do-or-die moment. If you asked your manager for a raise at an inappropriate time, the raise is not lost. You need to regroup. Build back the moment for the pounce. The next time you ask for the raise, you can refer to the previous request.

"Remember a couple of months ago when we discussed merit increases? Well, I'd like to revisit that conversation. However, I have a different proposition …"

Or

"Remember two months ago, I asked about distributions and how you would assess the team? I had an alternative thought that I wanted to go over with you …"

This will show persistence and confidence that you have an issue that will not go away and needs to be considered.

You thought walking would be easy and worthwhile, otherwise you would not have bruised your bum so often trying to walk. The pounce is worth it. Mastering the pounce theory will propel your career, education, romance, and your life forward. Living obliviously, like most do, is easy and will not bruise your ego, but it will also not allow you to walk and then run through life. You will always crawl. Always move forward. Pick yourself up after a failed pounce and rejoice that you have learned something for the next time.

Moving On

Once you have tasted success, you will not be content with less. However, dwelling on your success will only cause stagnation or bring you down. Assess your success, not only the outcome, but how you achieved it. Once you feel you can replicate the pounce, look forward to the next move. The next move may be the next step in your career, or the next step in a relationship, or even the next step in a negotiation of some kind. Dwell on your victory, and it will be short lived. Look into the future, and you will be content with your current success, but you will start the process of your next pounce.

There will come a time when you will have mastered your current situation and you will want to move forward. By looking forward the minute you have accomplished a goal, you will work toward the next goal more effectively. Things will come more fluidly and rapidly. If you dwell on your success for a month or a year, you will take on the role as if you will be there forever. After a while, you may get pigeonholed into the role and get bogged down for a considerable amount of time, more than you wanted.

Say you pounced on a new job opportunity and got what you asked for. Terrific! Celebrate that evening with a good dinner out on the town. However, once you have recognized yourself for your accomplishment, look at the next career move you would most likely make. As you go forward in your new job, your next step may change; however, by looking at the next move right away, you start working in a different manner. You associate with different people in the workplace. You will most likely present yourself in a different manner so as to set yourself up for the next move—the next pounce. It's amazing how quickly opportunities come when you are positioned correctly for them. If your new employer knows that you want a career path in a certain area of the company, as people leave or situations arise, you will be on their minds.

Again, the key to the pounce is planning ahead and learning not to jump when a situation arises, but instead to have yourself in the driver's seat for when it does. By looking forward and showing a humble self in your current position, you will put yourself in a good position for the next pounce. This will work for any type of relationship, career move, or negotiation. Stay humble and thankful for where you are at, but make your intentions known and watch for the opportunities when they appear.

The Last Takeaway

I've personally held numerous positions in management, from publically traded companies to government and law enforcement. I've taught management and leadership skills at the university level and in the private sector for companies in many marketplaces. What I have learned is there are many ways to pounce on an opportunity. The great part of analyzing a pounce is that there is a clear outcome: goal successfully achieved, or mission failed. There is a game plan and desired outcome. You were either successful or not. This is how managers and leaders are judged. What I like to look at is not the final outcome, but the setup and delivery.

Learn from your past pounces. This point cannot be stressed enough. You know what you need to look for, and you know what you desire. You have a good understanding of your surroundings and how others may react to you. Most likely, you have accomplished many things in your life up to this point. Understand your strengths, and move forward with those in mind. Don't dwell on your weaknesses or try and overcome them. Use your personality strengths, and look at your delivery. If you are a strong individual, ask for what you want directly. If you are less comfortable with a direct approach, guide the conversation with questions to get to the point you would like to make and have the other party offer. Whatever your strengths are, work within them and understand how you can most effectively pounce.

What you are looking for is refinement and better outcomes when you negotiate, advance in your career, or create relationships of any kind. Full refinement will not come from a book, a coach, or any sort of instructions, but these can be tools to help guide you. True self refinement can only come from within. Study what you have achieved. Study what others have accomplished and how they accomplished their goals. So often we focus on the end result. We look at how successful others are and what they have to show for it, but we do not know or truly understand how they got there. We assume or fabricate stories. Often we hear about exaggerated stories of terrible hardships and overcoming odds when, in fact, an opportunity arose and the individual pounced at the right time. These brief success stories have a lot of history to them. There was a method, a plan, and a goal that someone had. The journey had curves and turns, but there was always forward progress and finally success.

Look at your journey in life. How did you get where you are? You've had successes and failures. How did those occur, and what did you learn from them? Where do you want to go that is within your reach? We may all want to be rock stars, professional athletes, astronauts, or someone spectacular in the media; however, if you're thirty-five years old or older, you're not going to make the Lakers' first team. Of the options within your grasp, what do you want to get out of life? Make a reverse schedule. Pick a target date of when you want to complete certain accomplishments, and work backward from there. Concentrate on the setup. What will it take to research, understand, make the right contacts, and be the best and most prepared for reaching your goal? If you plan well, the pounce will appear. Good preparation will ensure a successful pounce.

With martial arts, you practice certain moves for years so that if an event occurs where you need to defend yourself, your brain is trained to react in a scripted and well-rehearsed manner. In much the same way, plan your pounces. Practice your talk tracks and dialogues and observe your surroundings to ensure your plan will not get derailed. Luck is not what made others successful. The harder one works, the luckier one gets. Study your accomplishments, look forward to the next—be patient, but be ready. The next pounce is there; do you see it?